OUT SIDE THE XY

A bklyn boihood
Anthology edited by
Morgan Mann Willis

For more information contact:
Riverdale Avenue Books
5676 Riverdale Avenue
Riverdale, NY 10471.

www.riverdaleavebooks.com

Design by www.formatting4U.com

Cover Art by Mickalene Thomas

Cover Design by Mekhi Baldwin and Scott Carpenter

Digital ISBN: 978-1-62601-303-2
Print ISBN: 978-1-62601-304-9

First Edition August 2016

Table of Contents

V. Sex

VI. Movement

VII. Mother/\Earth

VIII. Healing

Editor's Note

This anthology is an offering. In it we share ourselves as humans, as queer bois, studs, butch babies, transmen, aggressives, tombois, the intersexed, stealth, gay, non-cisgendered men, brotherboys, women, machas, butches, lesbian, femmebois, unlabeled, ungendered and unboxed. We are a collection of people whose voices and reflections are stories that commemorate the human experience through the delicate lens of self-affirmation and honest reflection. Outside the XY is a quilt.

These stitched together pieces span the range of time and space; contributors to this collection are black and brown. We hail from several continents—Africa, South America, Europe, North America, and Australia. We range in age, academic background, ability and identity. Some of us write, others are just beginning our journey with words. We are poets, academics, retail workers, hustlers, organizers, students, professionals, entrepreneurs and hybrids. We are immigrants, dual citizens, outsiders, roamers and in exile. We are disabled, cyborgs, able-bodied, chronically ill and healers. Some of us have never read an anthology. Some of us have never told our stories. Everyone in this collection is brave and has been generous with the fabric of their hearts.

1

Masculinity is not the thread that connects our work. We are joined in our journey of re-learning that masculinity is not defined by men, or by patriarchy, or television, or its apparent need to consume and produce violence. Masculinity is an umbrella in the sky of identity. Some of us live underneath its vastness centrally. Others of us have found pieces of who were are there, key pieces that help us see and know ourselves more clearly. Our relationship with and in masculinity is not rooted in any singular desire—aesthetic or sexual. We know that who we are simply *is* and requires no explanation. If you are looking for answers you may or may not find any here—this collection is sewn together by the struggle and progress of simply being alive.

bklyn boihood is so honored to work with Don Weise, our editor, and Magnus Books, the LGBTQ imprint of our publisher, Riverdale Avenue Books, and to have been given the space to curate this anthology in a way that felt inclusive and accessible to our community. We light candles on the regular for it to go far and wide.

As the Lead Editor, I'd like to thank my collective, my family, my brothers, my team, for allowing me the opportunity to recruit, review, gather, select, edit and compile this book. As a writer and community organizer, this feels like some of the most important work I will ever do. I am a Black, gay, woman, boi and gender non-conformist. My pronouns are she/they. I come from a long, long line of people who have determined masculinity for themselves. May this collection make them proud. Asé.

Morgan Mann Willis
Lead Editor

Introduction
(by Toshi Reagon)

I woke up this morning and I could see and I could breathe.
Are there any rights I'm entitled to?
—Bernice Johnson Reagon

Seems like since the day I was born I've known my name. The day I woke up seeing and breathing, I knew who I was and my declaration hit the air and rebounded across playgrounds, in classrooms, in vehicles, at multiple gatherings with family, friends, and strangers. Sometimes questioned but eventually affirmed because I would have it no other way. The only label I ever truly claimed was/is my name. My name is what comes with this body as she works the world. I sometimes blend into categories of my experience—Singer, Composer, Mom, Cultural Instigator, Producer, Curator, Freedom Fighter, Uncle, Pops, Papa, Husband, Boyfriend, Daddy, Friend but all of these names sit inside my given/chosen name.

It is a great gift to know who you are and why, even if that knowing is constantly evolving. Maybe that is why we live in a world so thirsty to disintegrate that great knowledge, so fast to devalue and so quick to try to unsteady that which cannot and won't be denied. Here in these pages is testimony to the truth of the matter that many folk knowing who they are and standing in that knowing and broadcasting from that knowing brings a strength and celebration to all who walk the world. This knowing broadens our possibilities and leans us in forward motion as it unsticks us from the mud of oppression.

I was three when I told my mom I did not like to wear dresses. She stopped putting them on me. I was so lucky that my mother was/is a civil rights activist and had some experience with folks stepping outside the lines that were created for them. When my mom joined the movement, she stopped straightening her hair. She started wearing buba's (African blouses). She scared her own mama. When I started playing football with neighborhood boys at eight, I started my lifelong love affair with my favorite uniform—T-shirt, jeans, boots or hi-tops. My mom worried and questioned this. My Aunt Mae Frances told my mother I was no different from her. My mother not only let me be but participated in my path by helping to expand my way.

My mom and I are both musicians. I grew up on the songs my mother taught me and on the musical soundtrack of my life growing up in Atlanta, Georgia and Washington DC. I learned about "I" songs. The text and poetry of "I" songs became additions to the line on which I write my name.

I'll Overcome
I'm Gonna Stay on the Battlefield
This Little Light of Mine (I'm Gonna Let it Shine)
I'm Gon' Stand (We will not bow down to Racism,
Injustice, Exploitation)
Say it loud- I'm Black and I'm Proud
I Was Born This Way

I become the first step to the possibility of a we, of a collective, of a movement, of a people. These pages are additional verses to these I songs. They join the long line of Black and Brown people declaring their names in a world sometimes not willing to hear the call. It makes no difference if the world is ready to hear or not. You still got a right to be and to declare your journey and your place in this world.

Toshi Reagon

Memory

The Unseen Boys

We've been gestating in this place for months. Slowly gaining our mannish figures. Leaning out, toughening up, filling in. Seeking pillar-like strength, maintaining cat-like abilities. We, the unseen boys that roam slowly into friendships and in with lovers, moving away silently, stealthily. We were never there to begin with, so why say goodbye.

These silent, thoughtful boys. Forced to introspection by loneliness.

You can't help but fall in with these boys, fall into their smiles. Love cemented by impatient eyes and forever gentle hands.

Let me tell you about these unseen boys.

They are held together by paste and tape, bound and stitched and waiting. Waiting without patience but with knowledge that nothing is coming, neither slowly nor quickly.

In this house we have each other. This is our Neverland, we are the lost boys. All brought by different pipers.

I met Ollie a few years before. They were so young, we were both so young. We lived in house on campus. I don't remember meeting them. I remember the time before I knew them and the time after.

9

It was like a friendship I had returned to but not from this life.

They were sitting on the porch when I got home, their head resting between their legs. Sorrow needed no explanation in this place we shared, but still, I was never good in moments like these.

I walked up to them and sat. The bench wasn't very long and our legs squished together a bit, the curls of hair linking at the tips.

I placed my palm on their back and felt warm sweat through their cotton shirt.

What do friends do for friends? How do they make the world easier?

I tip my shoulder toward them, a gentle nudge. They look at me. A slight shine in their resigned eyes. They kick my foot. We begin to walk. And slowly, following the path I run down every night. We begin to run straight, and when we can't breathe anymore, a park appears.

It belongs to the Korean church. Small and dimly lit.

I climb over the short green fence and they follow. I sit on the swing and they sit.

We kick off. The chain creaks loudly, normally with headphones on, I don't hear the park at night, I just sense the silence. But now I hear myself, and them. The sound of our legs pumping the air, the sound of the chains whipping back and forth as we climb higher and higher.

I work my legs harder, the swing bending tighter into me and pushing me away as I reach the peak.

With a slight sway our chairs collide and we become aware of each other in our reverie.

And here we lose control of ourselves, give in completely to the magic of this object surrounding us.

With a leap I come off the swing, and just as quickly, they are behind me, and we are running. Up the ramps and round the bars. Swinging and climbing, sometimes groping and grabbing at each other as we compete for access.

But in all its intensity it is gentle, laughs and grunts are the only communication. I roll awkwardly down the slide and they come tumbling down behind me. We collide on the turf, our heads whack together painfully. But we laugh. We laugh and smack each other a few more times before taking off. I feel the pull of Velcro under my shirt come undone, but it doesn't matter, I keep running, chasing after them. I climb up the rope and they are standing in front of the ship's wheel at the top of the tower.

The game is clear.

I begin to secure a sail and we start calling commands to each other. It is seamless, every movement in character. They call to me to ready the cannons, we must prepare for pirate ships in sight.

I watch them gracefully slide down the fireman's pole and onto the lower deck. I begin to descend.

I am still that child of eight. Or am I that child again?

A second time.

A second birth, a second growth.

We are boys.

Together. In our private silent moments, in our whispers about lovers.

We made each other boys, soothing stillborn childhoods. We flexed muscles, slouched and watched our bodies compressed into forms we openly desired but secretly questioned.

In our moments together we let ourselves regress to a place we had never been.

We admitted to lifting weights topless in binders, to shortened breaths and bruised ribs. We recognized it was worth it all. We wore sheepish smiles around pretty girls and watched suspiciously at men who flirted with them.

We were boys not Men.

We skinned our knees and waited for puberty.

-S Kamran

"Dear Ryann... Dear Ashley"

Dear Ryann,

Do you know how utterly amazing I think, no wait, I know, you are? Did you even know
you are my hero, a constant source of inspiration and motivation? Do you know how the thought of you makes me giggle and the sight of you leaves me breathless? Do you know how addictive your presence is? Don't laugh... or worse, don't be offended but I wish at *least* one of my kids is queer. If it means that someone will feel about them the way I do you and they have half the strength and character you do, then a thousand times yes, I want them to the queerest things ever to walk the Earth.

It takes an extraordinarily gifted soul to graciously rise above the dogma of what we are "supposed" to be; to take the garbage the world throws and create beauty. Do you know how wonderfully envious I am that the Universe chose you to bestow that gift upon? Think about that for a moment. How awesome must the Creator have known you would be? How bright the light emanating from your being must be if you were chosen before you were even created.

Your queerness (that doesn't seem like a word) is a gift, almost like a badge of worth. Not many of us are equipped or worthy to handle the manifestations of such an endowment. Wow... I love you even more now.

It's easier for me to see and appreciate now that I am older. When we were younger, I didn't know enough about myself to appreciate you. I didn't know that your light doesn't dim mine; its reflection actually helps my light shine brighter. The negativity and disdain you come across is people not knowing how to brighten their shine using yours.

I am pretty sure you already know all of this stuff about yourself. I just wanted you to know that I know... sorry it took me so long.

With all the love in my heart,

Your Sister, and Coincidentally Your Biggest Fan

--

Dear Ashley,

I remember our childhood and think about how confused I was most of the time. It's still hard for me to believe that that part of our lives is over. There was never a dull moment with the five of us in that house, and you always stood out to me as the leader. Not the oldest, but clearly a matriarch in training. I watched you go through so much of the shit that it takes for character to be born. You stood up for yourself and what you believed in no matter what. You were my loner/stoner sister, with great style and the coolest shit to say all the time. Only a few close friends, but you all clearly stood apart from the rest. I took my share of ass whippings from you too, but you would fuck anybody up or messing with me. Totally fair.

I can't believe you're a mother of three little queens now. You are doing such a wonderful job raising them. Your strength and love for your kids is beautiful. Not only are they lucky enough to have the coolest mom on the planet, they get to have a best friend, that they can trust with their fears, hopes, and dreams. They're amazing children, and I can't wait to see what the do with the world we leave them.

I feel so thankful to have you in my life.

I promise you, I wouldn't be who I am today, if it wasn't for your affirmation, and unconditional love. You've always seen me, and made me feel like I could be my whole self with no shame. That's big for a kid who used to "pray the gay away" every morning when I woke up for years. I wake up these days with my heart full.

I love you dearly,

Makenzi

Chicanada

Being hood means being chicano. I come from weekend barbecues of lowriders, guns, pachucos and cholos. The pachucos, their hands in their pockets, right and left kicks pointing outward and loose fitted pants-waist up is my culture. Masculinity isn't only the pachucos it's the hynas, las hermanas, the primas with the thick eyeliner. The tatted lipliner, eyebrows and Marilyn Monroe mole tats. Mi cultura is masculinity. Our persistent attitude masked by toughness is layers of years, 500 to be exact, of racism and colonial oppression. We masculinized who we are to preserve our calaberas, our tongue and our historia. Sixteen year-old Layel was asked to perform power and 26 year-old Layel was trying to perform authenticity. *Mi poder es mi masculinidad. Es como se cuida la cultura.* I am not trans-masculine. I am Muxe—our indigenous third gender that has opened many opportunities for all gender non-conforming Mexicans.

-Layel Camargo

Days of Awe

Temple Solel
Predominantly Black Jewish Congregation
Augusta, Georgia

I bound my chest on the holiest day of the year. It was Yom Kippur, the final day of Rosh Hashanah.

On Erev Yom Kippur, the morning prior, I went to Temple Solel to cleanse my sins. In the courtyard, surrounded by screaming families and muttering rabbis, I performed the holy ritual of Kapparot, rolling five-dollar bills into a handkerchief and then swinging it over my head. I chanted, "This is my exchange, this is my substitute, this is my expiation." Then I stuffed the bills into the communal charity box. Afterward, I sat on the stairs outside the synagogue and cried.

Someone placed a hand on my shoulder and then wrapped her arms around me. "Hey, why are you upset? What's wrong?"

"Nothing."

"Are you lying to me on Yom Kippur? God might strike you for that."

It was Maya; I knew her voice, I knew her touch, I knew the softness of her hands as she rubbed my back. All around us, people were walking around the courtyard, spinning money and calling, "This is my exchange," and, "He will bring them out of darkness and the shadow of death." I closed my eyes to pretend they weren't there.

Maya held my hand. "Do you want to tell me something?"

"Something like what? Of course not. What would make you think that?"

"You usually don't perform Kapparot. Last year, you didn't even come to temple on Yom Kippur."

"I was probably sick."

"You stayed home playing Call of Duty."

I averted my eyes. "I'm definitely coming this year," I said. "I'm coming to temple. I have to."

Maya raised her eyebrows. "Have to?

"Should."

She gazed at me for a moment longer and then looked away, which I appreciated, because she always knew when to leave me to my thoughts. She stretched out her legs, and her round thighs shone in the sunshine. I wanted to squeeze them. I also wanted to pull her into my lap and massage her shoulders; I could run a hand up her shorts, maybe even kiss the sweat from her—

"Elah?" she said.

"Huh—what? Yes?"

Maya picked at the loose threads in her shorts. "Are you still worried about what you told me last week? That you feel like God hates you?"

"No, it's not that."

She frowned. "I'm not worried.

"I've got it all worked out," I said, and cleared

my throat. "Do you want to come over for dinner tonight? My sister is making challah."

"I don't know," she said, "I feel like I should spend tonight with my own family."

Holidays at Maya's house were always difficult, because her father was an Ethiopian Jew and her mother was a Southern Baptist, splitting the house over holidays like Rosh Hashanah, Yom Kippur and Sukkot. I was trying to be nice by inviting her to my house, where at least everyone was culturally Jewish, even if we didn't always believe what we prayed. Actually, I was more than just being nice, I also wanted the chance to slip a hand up her shirt and place challah on her tongue.

I shook the image away. "Let me know if you change your mind."

"I will," and she squeezed my hand.

* * *

Yom Kippur was the Shabbat of Shabbats, a complete day of rest—and trying to rest was always hard work. When it came to Jewish law, I usually preferred to uphold the spirit instead of the letter. This time, however, I had to be strict to ensure that God forgave all of my sins; given the enormity of the transgression I was about to commit, I wanted to do it with a clean slate. I'd already lost points because my family decided to eat a second dinner instead of attend the evening service, but God would understand, hopefully. Yom Kippur officially started at sundown, so as soon as I glimpsed the palest pink light of sunset, I leaped up from the table.

My mother set down her fork. "Sit down, young lady, until everyone finishes eating."

"I need to go to Maya's house."

"Bring her some challah!" said my sister. "I only burnt half of it."

"She won't have time to eat it before tosefet."

"Give it to her mom." I rolled my eyes, but my mother said,

"Actually, that's a lovely idea," so I rolled the leftover bread in foil and carried it underneath my arm on the way to Maya's house. She lived several blocks away. I would have driven, but it's forbidden to drive on Shabbat and I didn't want to leave my car in her driveway for 24 hours.

When I rang the doorbell, Mrs. Fradkin opened the door and blinked down at me, rubbing at the bags beneath her eyes. Her hair was braided, but she had Maya's sharp jawline, Maya's full lips.

"Oh. Hi, Ellen," she said, using my American name.

"G'mar hatimah tovah," I said, "May you be sealed for a good year."

"I'll get Maya."

I stepped inside the foyer and rested the challah on the table while Mrs. Fradkin disappeared up the stairs. Maya came down a moment later, dressed in white, her curly brown hair tucked into a bun. She smoothed out the wrinkles in her dress and asked, "Did you want to go for a walk or something? Watch the sunset?"

Did I want to? Of course, especially since her hair still smelled like strawberry conditioner and I wanted to bury my face in it. But I had to say no. "I can't stay long. I just wanted to stop by and wish you well during Yom Kippur."

"Tzom kal to you too. Are you sure everything's okay?"

I nodded—but that was a lie, so I corrected myself. "Well, I will be. I will be okay."

"Do you want to talk?"

"I just need to say some extra prayers tonight. I need to do a lot of thinking."

She frowned. "That's what the Day of Atonement is for, I suppose.

"Pray for me."

"Of course. For what?"

I hesitated. On one hand, I wanted to melodramatically collapse to my knees, grab her hands and confess everything. Confess that some days, she meant more to me than God ever would. Confess that an overwhelming wrongness lived inside of me and made me sick of my own body. Confess that I was born wrong and needed her support to correct it.

Maya leaned toward me. "Hey, still there?"

"Just pray, okay?" I squeezed her hand. Then I sprinted home, already violating the no-physical-exertion rule of Yom Kippur. I stopped on my front porch, collected myself enough to walk inside, and went straight to my room. Trying not to cry. Trying not to cry. I crawled into bed. I stuffed the corner of my blanket into my mouth and bit down and told myself to pull it together. Don't scream. I screamed anyway, and bit down harder. Was I really going to go through with it? You can do this. I took two Nyquil and tried to fall asleep.

That night, I went to bed a woman, and I woke up a man.

Okay, that's not exactly how it happened. In fact, it was completely backwards: As usual, I went to bed

21

feeling like a man and woke up in the body of a woman, as I had for 17 years. Some people would call me transgender, while others would claim I was a man trapped in a woman's body, but the truth was much more complicated. Was I really born with the brain of a man? Maybe, or maybe not. Until second grade, my favorite game was princesses. But at age 13, when I watched all of my male friends become men at their bar mitzvahs, a shadow started to swallow me. For several days after each bar mitzvah I couldn't sleep and sometimes I wanted to throw up. All I could think was, "That should be me. That should be my ceremony." It took me four years to figure out that I didn't just want the bar mitzvah, I wanted the manhood.

Now I was going to get it. Yom Kippur started the new year with a new resolve: I was finally ready to start looking like myself. It would be an arduous, hellish process, but the first step was binding my chest. I could do that. Simple. Right? Heart pounding from a strange cocktail of terror and excitement, I knelt to pull a box from beneath my bed.

I unwrapped the tissue paper and removed the black chest and torso binder, which looked like a toddler-sized tank top. I tried to stretch out the material, but it had no give, and I remembered the warnings: Binding your chest will crush your ribcage. It will suffocate you.

I stood, inhaled deeply and then squeezed my upper body into the constrictor, which was ten times tighter than a sports bra and covered everything from my breasts to my stomach. I coughed—gasped for breath—felt suddenly lightheaded—but it had to be tight, or else it wouldn't flatten my chest.

I turned to the side in the mirror: The binder didn't flatten me completely, but the difference made me smile. Too bad the binder was black and not white, for Yom Kippur. I laughed at the absurdity: You know you're Jewish when God disapproves more of the color of your clothing more than whether you want to change your sex.

Over the binder, I buttoned up a white shirt and matching slacks. Instead of letting my hair curl into a girlish afro, I dipped a comb in water and parted it to the side, then scrutinized myself in the mirror. "Not bad," I whispered, not because I believed it but because I wanted to convince myself. If anything, with my wide black eyes and monkey's ears, I looked like a 13-year-old boy.

I knelt again beside my bed to pray. What could I say? Asking God to bless me in the face of sin would be a disgrace, so I simply mumbled, "Dear God, do not strike me down today. I'm only trying to become the man that I was born to be."

-J. Tomas

Victoria Carmen White

A, Parker T Hurley

Several events converged throughout my life that have connected me to the lightness and darkness of humanity and continue to transform me as well as my identity as a queer, mixed-race, black, non-binary transman. However, few of the moments that are guided by nationally felt devastation incited by violence or natural disasters, have been as powerful in my development than the incremental ways that I have been told that I am not enough and conversely how intrinsically worthy I truly am. My lived-experiences has undeniably been shaped by the micro-aggressions against me tended by my conscious and unconscious mind, as well as a collective awareness that as queer, black, brown trans bodies we are considered superfluous, criminal, pathological and disposable.

   As someone who has made gender a constant study, who moves through and combines masculinity and femininity between inhales and exhales; it is no accident that I chose to be a social justice educator and to live as an activist. I engage in this work as a necessity for my own survival. From as early as I can remember,

I have been painstakingly aware of the disparities that exist in our society. Raised in New Jersey by a single white mother ill-equipped to raise twin brown babies, I once believed that being the product of an interracial union and their incongruent love, somehow typified what it meant to be "different." However, it was not until I came out as a dyke at the age of 16, and then again, as transgender at 24, that I truly began to learn the extent to which society has the capacity to divide people into the categories of "normal" and "other," and the material consequences of living and identifying outside of a dominant culture. I have come to think of my experiences as a mixed-race person, of learning how to navigate a country obsessed with boundaries and binaries, as my prerequisite for learning how to be transgender in a cis-sexist world. As a mixed-race young person, I instinctively knew that somewhere over the proverbial rainbow a life existed outside of black/white, man/woman, masculine/feminine, straight/gay binaries. From the first time I was forced to check a box on a standardized test at school signifying whether I was black or white (multi-racial was not a category in the 80's), I knew that there would never be a box that would fully encapsulate who I am.

Schooling remains one of the mainstays of socialization and often maintains the values and practices of dominant culture. Through a critical lens, education is not just a microcosm of the larger racist, classist, sexist, xenophobic, heteronormative culture, reflecting disdain for the other but it is performative and regulatory in nature. It was at a predominately student of color elementary school that I have some of my earliest memories growing up identifying as "mulatto" to describe my mixed-race heritage (a word offered to me by my teachers and hungrily received by my then eight, nine, and ten year-old self, never knowing what it really meant). The identity followed me even to a more racially and economically diverse middle and high school.

The story of my formal education as a mixed race student included lessons around "code-switching," how to complete the "family tree" project without my entire history relayed to me, and navigating the social obstacle course that was the self-segregated cafeteria. School is where I first learned that I wasn't black enough or white enough. School is also where I learned that I wasn't girl enough. School is where I learned to pass. School is also where I learned about power. School is where I became politicized.

School is also where I met Victoria Carmen White. She spoke about her struggle coming of age as a teenage girl including menstruation cramps, fashion, and boy troubles in addition to the milieu of high school classes, tests, rehearsing for the school play. Unlike many high school girls and like me, Victoria was transgender. Unlike me, Victoria shared her struggle with her gender openly. Her openness was too perilous for most people to acknowledge, even myself as a now out and proud queer, transman of color. I wanted her to go away, to not flaunt herself; I wanted her to keep her silent so that I could be comfortable. At the time, I didn't want anyone to think that I was like Victoria Carmen White.

Although neither of us left high school unscathed, our transgressive gender expressions incited hostility from teachers and administrators alike, our stories quickly diverged. As trans masculine person, I worked to connect with the burgeoning queer that I was to build a support system of teammates, counselors and a select group of teachers, the school administrators forbade me to take any of the only out butch dyke teacher's classes, in fear of his influence over me. Like many masculine of center students of color, especially those of us who were queer, my guidance counselor told me to forgo any aspiration towards college and to "settle" on a trade and subsequently refused to work with me.

These tensions and the stress of being visibly queer, combined with a home life saturated with emotional and physical abuse erupted on my transcript. Although at the end of my senior year I was named a High-School All-American lacrosse player, I only graduated with a 1.7 GPA. However, Victoria, like many trans women of color, didn't have another trans woman for a teacher and never graduated from my high school, but rather was ushered by the school administrators to an "alternative" school and I never heard of her again until the news of her murder almost a decade later. On September 12, 2010, her killer ended her life by shooting her to death in a neighboring town in New Jersey, when she was only 28 years old.

Unlike Victoria, I survived; that same butch teacher became a parent to me, he is where my Irish last name comes from, and he presently remains the only out butch dyke teacher at my high school, despite the influx of queer youth. He works relentlessly every day for all of his students to express themselves and creates spaces that are affirming and conducive to learning. He and the rest of my chosen family are the reasons why I was propelled to search for my own histories, flag, and communities that reflected more of who I was in the world. I was fortunate enough to have counselors, friends and teachers to support me in these endeavors. And at the end I found that as a queer, trans person of color, I come from a long ancestry of warriors who worked in resistance to the status quo (hetero or homo normative). And it is in our collective struggle that I continue in my journey as a doctoral student, community organizer and social justice educator.

To learn the stories of my ancestors and to write and share my own is as daunting as it is liberating. Moreover, to engage in social justice education and any kind of liberation work is to entertain the paradoxical nature of having to relate first to the injustices and oppressions that we are working to eradicate. Collectively and individually we are called upon to "grapple with" the magnitude of centuries of interwoven histories and events that have resulted in the social, political and economic stratification of humanity; more than often equating to life for some and death for others. It is not a coincidence that most poor people in this country who receive public assistance are white; still the image of the black, single-mother welfare queen still persists in our minds, policy and practices. Similarly, it is not a coincidence that the prisons are filled with men of color, that most students tracked in lower level classes are youth of color, or that although "the LGBTQ community" is often depicted as one homogenous people and that it is queer and trans people (trans women of color in particular) who are sick, imprisoned, detained, deported, unemployed and murdered.

Even still, it is not a coincidence that we aren't taught the names of trans women of color who resisted police brutality, inciting the Stone Wall Riots, such as Sylvia Rivera, Marsha P. Johnson and Miss Major who unapologetically fought for the economic and social justice of queer, trans and gender non-conforming people; or that these same trans and queer people of color rarely in leadership positions within LGBTQ non-profit and advocacy organizations. The insidious nature of system oppression is made evident by the reality that the histories of oppressed people have been omitted, truncated and erased; entire knowledges and epistemologies are continuously being subjugated and de-legitimized; while white, imperialist, heteronor-mative, patriarchy is naturalized and reified as the cultural barometer against which all else is measured. My personal and professional experiences as a transman of color have urged me to become intimately invested in the kind of information being disseminated, who gets taught and how they are taught.

It is also no coincidence then, that as a trans masculine person who has engaged for over a decade in liberation/social justice work that I still feel uncomfortable with calling myself a "leader," and, more often than not, feel like an imposter. As a poor person, a first generation college student, a queer person, as a black person, I rarely see people like me in leadership positions. Transparently, even in writing this piece, I have had an increasingly difficult time being self-reflective because my narrative diverges from the archetypal ones I absorbed about what it means to be a "well-adjusted" mixed-race person, or because as a queer, transman I have not always known that I was trans and have never considered myself "a man trapped in a woman's body." When I thought of my own feelings and narrative, I would often conjure up thoughts and emotions that are depicted through mainstream media and promoted through the stories we even tell each other (i.e. confusion or conviction, self-hate, or complete self-actualization "post-operatively"), none of which I have felt extensively. Problematizing and ultimately moving away from one-size-fits-all identity politics have become a large part of the work that I do every in the hopes of producing counter-narratives that tell the stories more fully of how I live, falter and resist.

To this end, my assemblage of identities as a queer, mixed-race, black transman places me on an oppressor-oppressed continuum. I am someone who has historically known (and continues to know) the fear of walking down a street burdened by the omnipresent threat of rape and sexual violence and most recently I have experienced women flinching when I walk too close behind them on the sidewalk or cross the street as I approach. With the introduction of a beard and a deeper voice, I am now a reminder of their trauma, and target for their prejudices which forces me to reconcile who I have been, who I grow to be, and who it is that people perceive me to be almost every minute of the day.

There isn't any classroom, or pre-testosterone counseling session that prepared me for what it means to become America's boogieman; a black man. What I was first acquainted with as a gender non-conforming dyke and what was further illuminated after engaging in hormone therapy and beginning to "pass" as a man of color, is that without organically derived psychological schemas, black masculinity is suspended in others' projections, desires/fantasies, or agendas.

Black masculine /black trans masculine bodies are positioned within a cycle of dehumanization, regulation, criminalization and mass execution. Unlike our white trans-masculine counterparts, we become tropes and are placed outside of our homes, families, communities, the academic industrial complex, the non-profit industrial complex and political life. We are thought of as phantoms, heroes or "let-downs," if we are thought of at all. The void caused by a non-essentialist collective history that prevents black masculine-of-center individuals from falling neatly into stratifications of criminals, gangsters, ballers, underdogs and heroes has us all trans and cisgender black men learning what it means to be men. To be black men. To be black masculine of center people that invest in a kind of masculinity that does not innately tethered to white-supremacist, heteronormative, capitalist, patriarchy.

Still, throughout my life, I often found myself complicit in the reiteration have this brand of masculinity. Having once been a dyke, raised in a household of women, and a former female athlete, I never aspired to be a man and still do not conceptualize myself in that way. My father's brief cameos in my life never provided much insight as to what was required of manhood and my mother's masculinity was brutish and emotionally vacant. As a butch dyke, I found myself regurgitating a brand of masculinity that was rigid, abusive and intense, while simultaneously chivalrous, cocky and aloof. I did everything I could to be perceived to be a threat to

31

other masculine of center people, especially non-trans men who asserted that my girlfriends were "too pretty to be gay," and were threatened by my fade, my swagger and our hand holding. My masculinity was the alarm signaled to the world that I was queer and it was the shield I needed because I was so visibly queer.

Over the years, I have seem to trade one kind of invisibility for another. As a transman, I no longer read as visibly queer, which saddens me because I go without the affirmation from butches and studs walking down the street just thinking that I am another guy who is interested for all the wrong reasons. But, now as someone who reads irrefutably as a "guy," I am no longer in the position of having to police my gender in the same way. Although historically black, hyper-masculine spaces like barber shops still remain to be places where I feel myself monitoring my expressions and having to make familiar negotiations around gender.

Similarly, I find myself feeling displaced by the hyper-masculinity and heteronormativity laden in trans masculine of center spaces and often suffocated by the trans misogyny and violence generated by those who might look like me but who locate their masculinity in the domination of women and femmes. It wasn't until years later and I began to assert myself as a queer, non-binary, transman and found others who identified similarly and were more invested in creating a more creative, sometimes malleable, transformative masculinity, that I began to love what it means to be in a room full of transmen and masculine of center people of color and share our thoughts, struggles and our personal histories. Together we share the weight of our black, transmasculine existence oftentimes being made to feel only as big as the obligations we are asked to fulfill and as strong as the responsibilities we are expected to carry. We share our frustrations with new ways of emoting when tears are not as accessible, and for caring for ourselves without the fear of being seen as conceited and too self-involved. We learn from and teach one another how to be heard, while balancing the privilege of being masculine (and therefore all-knowing) and the danger of performing black masculinities.

Still, I am repeatedly saddened by how few spaces are available to us to be ourselves, to doubt, to rage, or to cry and to collectively work towards a brand of masculinity that centers healing, care and interrupts misogyny and stands in solidarity with women and femmes. I have found these spaces few and far between. Even within the most progressive of activist circles it is a challenge to make space for my queer/trans masculinity and to assert myself as someone who is unwavering in my willingness to be transformed (which is often confused with uncertainty), as a leader that does not believe in hierarchies (which also is confused with uncertainty and incompetence) and as someone who is not always thrilled about the expensive, painful and inconvenience of undertaking a physical transition (which gets misconstrued with inauthenticity). I have also had to work extremely hard to combat the internalized capitalism that has me consumed with what I can do and how fast I can do it, instead of speaking to my intrinsic self-worth.

To be deemed a "good black man" is to perform outside of the inculcated, patriarchal narratives of criminals, gangsters, ballers, underdogs and heroes. At some point in my development, I found it hard to resist the allure of being neatly stratified into each of these categories. I lingered in being the "underdog" the longest. Considering, I survived a physically and emotionally abusive childhood, came out as gay at the age of 16 and after almost failing out of high school went on to become the first person in my family to graduate from college with a full athletic scholarship. A little more than ten years after my high school guidance counselor told me that I wasn't college "material and that I should "settle on a trade," I am working to complete a doctorate degree in Educational Studies, and living my life as an out, queer, trans person. And although this story makes me a statistical anomaly, I now know that I have never been, nor will I ever be, an underdog.

The underdog model also relies on the myth of meritocracy and does not shed light on the privilege I maintain as a light skinned, documented American, who does not have a disability, who is perceived to be male that propelled me through life. Making the distinction between my black trans-ness and that of a black trans-woman, is vital to movement building. I was able to pull from points of privilege to survive. Victoria did not have access to those same privileges. Moreover, what makes the story of the underdog, or hero, so dangerous is that these characters are seen as acting alone to overcome adversity. Or that adversity can always be overcome. Victoria cannot overcome being murdered.

The mythology of these elite protagonists described as extraordinary individuals that drew from some intrinsic and unrivaled wealth of strength and courage to "pick themselves up from their bootstraps," enough to incite longstanding social transformation is seductive and oftentimes anesthetizing. The perilous nature of the story of the underdog or hero is tied to a nostalgic and revisionist conception of history. To uphold histories of social movements that are ornamented with stories of iconic martyrs and unequaled heroes is detrimental to meaningful and sustainable liberation work because we cannot see ourselves and our everyday acts of resistance as equating to social transformation/history.

What being queer and being a part of social justice efforts in the US South has taught me is that a huge part of liberation work is to not see ourselves, our movements or our heroes as being not all good or bad. Liberation work can hurt like hell. I have been disappointed and emotionally abused within non-profit settings. I have burnt out and isolated within self-proclaimed radical, queer spaces. And I have been tokenized and left uncompensated for the work that I have done, more often than not. It definitely has not always been all "good." Moreover, I have been complicit in my power as a masculine presenting person in social justice movements. I have engaged in trans misogyny because I have not wanted to look directly at how I was replicating larger systems of oppression, because I myself was tired of being broke and disenfranchised and I thought I needed leadership at whatever the cost. Even if it meant black and brown transwomen having to wait for their compensation, until I was comfortable. I know now how problematic and shortsighted my thinking and behavior was.

Still, queers in the US South have taught me how to move away from a culture of disposability and to recognize that conflict and imperfection are to be expected and are required of revolution. I have learned that we all contain multitudes and hypocrisies and that change is slow moving. I've learned that reconciliation has to occur between the parts of our selves that are fragmented and wounded. And although we are all not all good, we are worthy of care and love from ourselves, our partners and our communities. Which means, that as gender non-conforming, trans people of color need to posit healing work as central to our leadership identity development. We contain centuries of trauma in our spirits and within our bodies that require attention.

For me, like Audre Lorde, self-care is not self-indulgence, it is self-preservation, and that is an act of political warfare." Trans justice movements must overlap with social justice efforts that lift up the power of community and practices of care within those communities. We have failed in many ways to take care of ourselves and our elders within social justice circles-creating unsustainable movements that specifically have trans* and queer activists of color working without being adequately compensated for their skill sets and efforts, leaving us more susceptible to burnout, poverty and isolation. To this end, I have always mistrusted the phrase, "standing on the shoulders of giants," because although I respect and pay homage to the brilliance and resilience of my ancestors, I'm fairly certain that they were not giants, but as powerful and as vulnerable as I am. We cannot afford to build movements based on icons, grandiosity and visibility in and of itself.

The fact of the matter remains; we don't need a messiah, a prince charming on a gleaming white horse, a hero, an underdog or be any of these characters to create the world in which we want to live in. We do, however, need to create more opportunities to be intimate, connected and more real with each other and ourselves. We need more teachers like my butch father who leverages their white privilege to empower students of color, not save them. We need to move past solidarity and allyship and demand that those with power, risk that power and interrupt the illusion of safety, comfort and equality. We need all of the women like Victoria Carmen White to live and to view the ending of violence against all women as the nexus of liberation.

For me to see myself as an agent of that change means crossing the finish line with all of me which includes: the girl, the boy, the queer, the survivor, the self-lover, the self-hater, the ex-partner, the adoptee, the twin, the misogynist, the healer etc. Presenting myself as being all brave, or all of anything robs myself and my communities from gaining access to me and the power of my truth. Living outside of binaries is something that has been gifted to me by my ancestors and I intend to employ all of myself to love all of us free.

-Parker T Hurley

Untitled

i first fell in love in new york.
i'd wait for her in the elevator.
with their backs turned, we'd hold each others hand.
that taught me that my love was a mask
no one should look at.

                       a few years later, i found love again.
                           she was older. a college girl.
                       told me all lesbians wear chucks,
                      swear i bought about every pair
                  that year. red, royal blue, navy blue,
camo, gray, custom made, even had some wool ones
               for the winter. that taught me that love is
                              a costume.

i was a virgin.

she said she wanted to change that.
but by the time she finished college
i had entered college and some other bitch
beat her to the punch.
i lied
my first time. told her she wasn't my first.
technically

38

i'd been practicing since kindergarten.
i didn't wanna face my past, instead
i earned a reputation for being a pimp.
That taught me that power has nothing
to do with who you are, but everything to do
with who you think you are. I thought
i was the man! I had girls in the palm of my hand,
literally. i was ass smackn and finger fuckn, unaware
that i was perpetuating the patriarchy.

Yea, I studied women's studies, but
what the fuck is feminism when butch gets bitches?
i was blindsided by snapbacks and sports bras,
discovered dominance in dildos,
related women with weakness. Defined submissive
as "femme". so i became
stud.
butch.
dyke.

control. power. dominant. dick.
i was arrogant. asshole. abuser. abusive.

the first time i slapped my girl
i admit
it felt good. she cried on the floor like a helpless toddler.

she said she hated me. i apologized
between her thighs. she said she loved me.

she said she loved me so much she hated herself.
she said she hated herself so much she couldn't love me
anymore.

i tried to make her love me, but it was useless.
that taught me that dick is useless without pussy.
what good is a key if she change her locks.
and how hard must you knock if she won't let you in.

i was no different than men with heterosexual privilege.
all my bitches

were victims. i realized i was a woman
regulating rape culture

every time i retrieved her number before retrieving her
name.
every time i expected sex at the end of a date.
every time i deemed myself playa as if her body was a
game.

i had to make a change.

she is me. we
are the same species.
i discovered manhood by slaying my ego.
being a man has nothing to do with having a penis.
being a man has everything to do with protecting women.
i am more man than some men.

will ever be.

-Maya Thompson

Dear Tito

When I think of my life as a masculine person, I think of sawdust, tools, heavy machinery and paint. I also think of colors and their relationship to light. I think of barbecues and times around the grill with the guys. I also think of the camaraderie and the safe spaces grilling gives us when we're feeling vulnerable and anxious. I think of my privilege of having physical strength and mobility to carry heavy things. I also think of the blessing to be able to hold heavy things in my heart and continue to love.

My relationship with masculinity was born before I understood what it was. Raised in a Filipino immigrant family, my house was filled with my parents, my sister, my Lola, my Tito Jun and sometimes other family members. My Tito Jun was the one who took care of me the most, being much more than an uncle to me. He passed when I was in high school from murdering his racist white boss and then committing suicide right after. This is my letter to him about the things I never got to talk to him about.

--

Dear Tito,

Firstly, I want to say how much I miss you. You passed so much sooner than any of the family thought you would. I always thought you'd be in my life, and I regret not appreciating the time I had with you. I never had the opportunity to come out to you as queer or as a transmasculine genderqueer. As I reflect on my life, I wonder what you would think of how I love the people in my life, my relationship with GABNet and the Philippines, and of all my queer/trans*/kinksters in my life. I have a feeling you would have loved them. I imagine that you'd be right there with my dad, joking and laughing, offering people drinks. I also have a feeling that you already knew, that this wouldn't be news to you. I remember you calling me a tomboy. It wasn't till 20 years later that I learned that tomboy is slang for a masculine presenting lesbian in Tagalog. Even if you did know, you loved me and never tried to change anything about me. Rather you embraced my desire to wear boy clothes and supported me and the many ways I wanted to be. You are an essential part of who I am now.

The moments shared with you are my first memories of masculinity. You worked so hard to provide for us, for Lola, my sister, my parents, your wife and children back home and for the rest of the family. You would come home smelling of gasoline with oil stains on your blue shirt. I feel like I honor that now when I come home smelling of paint and covered in sawdust exhausted from the day.

My home is filled with books, a love that you've implanted in me. I don't think I've ever told you how much I loved going to the flea markets every month, running around to find the one book for you to buy me. Even after your passing, I still buy books as self care. They still give me the same feelings of joy as when I was young and holding your hand through the stalls. The love of constant learning and growing from reading has definitely given me access to certain privileges and opportunities I know I wouldn't have had if it wasn't for our monthly flea market book trips and the time you dedicated to me.

One of my fondest memories is the day you taught me how to make filipino barbecue. You were hosting one of the many large parties you would throw. You always invited everyone ¬ family, extended family, strangers. Everyone was welcomed in your home. Everyone was a Tita or a Tito even if I didn't know their name. Feeling anxious from so many people around that I didn't know, I found comfort in standing next to you at the grill in the backyard surrounded by Lola's roses that you helped plant. You turned to me and asked if I wanted to learn. As I shyly nodded, you gently instructed me through the marinade process, explaining how much 7 Up to add so it could soften the meat while adding a little sweetness. You held your hands on top of mine as they held the tongs, helping me flip the sticks of meat. You were so generous with your gentle ways around me, being an example of how small gestures can give so much comfort to an awkward person.

I still find comfort by the grill today. A year ago there was a gathering for transmasculine people to come together and get to know one another. As it was a beautiful summer day, my friends were hosting and

43

decided to grill. My friend and I were greeting people as they came in, introducing ourselves and hoping to build community. As the small talk grew into conversations, we found ourselves feeling uncomfortable as people's internalized patriarchy started to began to show. To comfort each other, we turned to the grill, joking how, like our ancestors, we were now the old uncles standing at the grill complaining about everyone around us. We stood there for hours, even when there wasn't any more food to grill. The grill became our safe space, a place where we can reflect and share our hopes and desires for our friendships, love, and community.

While I didn't understand it back then, you were also kinky. It was in your basement where I found my first porn. You didn't hide it all; it sat on your shelves just like your plastic breasts were hanging on the wall and your mirrors were on the ceiling. Dad only ever said one line to me about sex. "I know you are having it, just make sure you are safe." I still don't understand how our family is so quiet about talking about sex while you displayed it proudly and loudly. I wonder if you would have given me the "sex talk" rather than dad.

There are so many things I could look thank you for but the most important value you've taught me was how to love, honor, respect, and listen to the women in our lives. Because of that I was able to open space in my spirit to receive wisdom from the femmes in my life. It was the femmes that really fine-tuned my masculinity. The femmes in my life are teachers, drummers, dancers, welders, photographers, architects, healers and so much more. They are the fire builders and the campers. The femmes gave me the ability to embrace my tenderness, compassion, giggles, softness, and love for small things. They were the ones who slowly and lovingly broke down the walls I built around my emotions and gave my feelings words and a voice. They showed me how to express my anger with love instead of aggression. Femmes were the ones that showed me militancy and the strength and resilience to fight for what we believe is right. Through example, they taught me how to hold all parts of a person in my heart, the struggles as well as the joy. They were the ones that led me to my kinks. I embrace my body and my whole self because of them.

Sometimes when I think of your passing, the anger you must have felt when you shot your boss, then the despair and agony in the realization of what you have done, I think of how I wish I could have been able to help. As a child I knew of your anger even if you never showed it to me in our time together. In time, I understand your anger as an immigrant, filipino man working for a white boss. I want to let you know this one action didn't define the whole of your life and wasn't worth your death. It makes me think of my own struggles with self-hate and the fight I had to love myself despite my flaws, mistakes and missteps. I think of my own anger and how to focus that on the change I want to see in the world and in my life. I wish we were able to share our anger, our outrage. I want you to know that because of all the love and wisdom you gave me, I was able to build substantial community of queer and trans people who share their beautiful light with so much strength and conviction that it continues to grow and nourish my own light and spirit. They provide the space for me to be angry, the

45

tools and support in which I can confront it and use it rather than keeping it bottled inside me.

I want you to know that I still love you, that there was nothing you have done that would negate that love. I want you to know that I hold you in my heart everyday and I am so grateful for having been raised by you.

loving you always. -e

-E. Armea

Untitled

I found queer, found trans, found gender-essentialism-is-bullshit rage when I was 15 years old, and it completely fucked me up. Had me thinking there was such a thing as "trans enough," even as I learned to reject the idea of being a "real man." Had me comparing myself to Kate Bornstein and Les Feinberg, even as I stopped answering voicemails from my father.

I learned the word "mulatto" at age 13. The word transgender at 15.

Each time, I grabbed those words with both fists, and ran. Identity became a commodity. Became expensive. Became shopping trips to buy boys' clothes I couldn't afford, became fucked-up ideas about who and how I should date, became the more-than-anything desire to hear "you're such a guy!" even though, sometimes, it stung. Masculinity, I thought—like beauty—must be painful, too. This is what it feels like to be enough.

I dated an abuser when I was 16. First, because he was gay. No, stop. Let's get specific: because he was cis and gay. Because of the way a cisgender gay man, insatiable for dick, was attracted to me, and this meant that I was enough. Like the kids who walked the runway, bragging about invisibility. The power to be unseen.

I learned, when I was 15, that you can't be queer and Black at the same time. This, despite the fact that I was queer and Black at the same time. Despite the fact that my mentors taught me different. The fact that drop-in centers and queer youth spaces on both sides of Eight Mile were filled with Black youth every Friday night. Despite the fact that I've always been my father's son.

The thing is, there are rules about being Black. We all know them. Learn them before anything else they teach us in school. We know all the ways to tell who's Really Black. Your voice over the phone. Your grades. Your bank account. Your car. Your zip code. Sagged jeans, Jordans, dew rags, and chains. Nuance costs, and all the Black kids are broke.

It was simple. Like math, which I also flunked.

Gender was new and exciting, when I was 15. If the cis-tem had traumatized me, then my survival had been dissociation. While other trans youth talk about the pain of puberty, I can honestly say I don't remember it. I know that age gave my body unwelcome significance, but oblivion kept me alive, so I can't tell you how it happened. I do know that, as soon as it hit me, I was on the ground running. Sprinting as fast and far as I could, away from everyone and everything that bound me, no matter the cost. So when something changed, and I was able to stop, the adrenaline must still have been pumping. It must still have been flushing through my veins. I was reckless in my newfound self-love. I was drunk on self-acceptance: a drug, especially to a queer kid who's never felt it before. This is what it feels like to be enough.

Power has always been precious. And the older I get, the more convinced I become that power lies where there are options.

At the same time, I know how badly choices can hurt, because I'm trans and mixed race. I grew up in two homes: one in the city, and one in the suburbs. And when I was 19, I lived in two countries, despite poverty, and against laws set up to stop me. It was terrifying, and not in an exhilarating way. So choice never felt like a luxury. Honestly, it seemed like a punishment. Still, though, that's what I think privilege is. I think privilege is choices.

I learned the hard way, when I was 15, that being trans was a choice.

Not the choice to reject my assigned gender. That came as naturally as breathing. But it was a choice to sacrifice my Blackness for something new. A choice nobody told me I was making. The more visible my queerness became, the more my color was called into question. The same ones who get called "faggot" on the playground are those who are told they "act white," and it's not a coincidence. Kids like us don't get to be both. We all know we're never enough.

It took years for me to realize what I had done. Years before rage reclaimed what white supremacy had stolen from me. In high school, white queer adults took me in. They loved me, and taught me trans boys could be femme. What they never told me was that only some of us can afford to reinvent masculinity. In order to reject a hegemonic manhood, we must, after all, have some claim to gender in the first place. As Black and brown queers, our departure from cis-tems of gender essentialism began when we were born into a white supremacist world. A world where we can never truly reject gender, since gender does not belong to us, in the first place.

These days, gender is about as familiar to me as any other part of white Amerikkka. That is to say, I live here, but make no mistake: this can never be my home. When I make choices ¬ about pronouns, about hair length, about whether or not to wear makeup, or how to dress, how to talk, how to walk ¬ these actions have little to do with validation or visibility. They are calculated risks. A route I chart myself. The mace in my pocket. The whistle 'round my neck. This is not about expression. This is about safety. About protection. About making it out alive, even when all this is still, somehow, not enough.

-Lance Hicks

island boi

I was 14.
with burnt black skin, standing in front of
my grandmother's mirror:
an island child, hair down and
window open
to let in curry heat
The towel fell:
I stood uncovered before the glass and
pinched my cheeks,
scraping wet hair from my forehead, and
working my jaw
angrily like Granddaddy did
I look like a boy,
I whispered to the steam that
folded upward from the
shower, and
I dug my fingertips into the mirror,
wishing I could bend glass
I did not wish to be a boy
at the time
but even then I sensed
that these budding breasts had grown

bklyn boihood

too heavy,
bending my spine
with their demands

-J. Tomas

Sacred Heart

Haiti 2002

"She's coming back to school today!"

It's the first thing I hear as I reach my group of friends. They are really talking about this again?

I almost roll my eyes. Well, at least once she's here, they'll be able to talk about something else.

It is seven- something in the morning, in the capital of the Land of Mountains, the sun fiercely claiming its place in the sky, is beating down on the school grounds, dare move too fast and you'll be sweating before the bell rings. There are hundreds of girls of all ages huddled in little groups, some sitting, some standing, all talking, trying to get in as much as possible before the bell rings. Somehow we never run out of things to talk about but today, in my group, they are only talking about her and I am standing with them, quiet, with nothing to add. I am relatively new to the group, our parents don't run in the same circles, I haven't grown up with any of them, I am in a precarious position, and the buzz about her homecoming makes me uneasy. Slightly uncomfortable in my thick grey skirt and my, thankfully thin white blouse, all of my insecurities flaring up, I sense the jealousy rising up inside of me with every glance they send towards the gates of our school. I am lost in my head, nervous, cowering at the thought of her arrival.

Really, I am ready for it to be over.

The time has come. Here she is. I see her walk in and she is thin, so very thin, big haired, awkward, and being assailed by MY friends. They are hugging her, kissing her, and if it wasn't for a sense of decorum, they probably would've put her on their shoulders and carried her around the schoolyard, Jewish wedding style. I find the outburst to be ridiculous.

After what seems like an eternity, they spread out around her and I can finally take a second look at her. When I see her, my heart unexpectedly begins to race at a dangerous pace, threatening to jump right out of my chest. I, of course, too cool to show how I am feeling, stay back and remain silent. She seems alright.

I am looking at her more closely now. Her thin frame is floating inside her blindingly white blouse, the thick black leather belt is sitting right under the belly button holding up the grey skirt stopping right under the knee—any longer and you enter dangerous territories of committing aCatholic school fashion faux pas—, the leather of her shoes without a crease, she is smiling but remaining quiet. I can't get over how thin she is, I imagine that a single hug from someone like me, tall for my age, thick legs and a slightly less thick upper body, could break her. So thin I want to hug her to see if she'd actually break.

I reluctantly take my eyes away from her and become once again aware of my surroundings. They are still fawning over her, making sure she understands how happy they are to have her back. They begin to move and I, as if I had suddenly gone mute, quietly follow them to our official hang out spot under the stairs of the chapel hidden from the sun. Despite all the chatter around her she remains calm, smiling and answering all the questions they are firing at her, not at all how I expected her to react. Hard to dislike someone who seems surrounded by walls, aloof, and so damn cool. I am at a loss on how to take her in. I lose control over my eyes once again and I begin to notice the finer details of her face: her eyelashes curling onto themselves revealing big brown eyes, a wide mouth that somehow fits perfectly with her bony nose, bushy eyebrows that almost meet in the middle, angular jaw attached to a bony neck, perfectly smooth brown skin. I can feel that I am being awkward. Damn, she is beautiful.

Haiti 2003

I have grown to like her. Alright, let me be honest. I have grown to become a complete ball of awkward mess around her. Everything she does seems extraordinary to me. She sketches and every doodle becomes an invaluable work of art in my eyes. She plays volleyball so some afternoons I abandon my basketball practice to go play with the volleyball team. Our friends are beginning to notice. I am physically affected by her presence. My breathing gets shallow, I sweat just a bit more, I can't think in complete sentences, I want to disappear. I find her overwhelmingly beautiful and I can't stop looking at her. I am always afraid someone will see me staring at her. Now that I think about it, only an army of deaf and blind teenage girls would have been able to ignore my dangerous fall. I want to do everything for her because I desperately want her to like me. I praise her brilliance to all who would listen but sometimes, only sometimes, I hate her.

I am beginning to understand that I am not like the other girls in my class. I start to push back in every way. I categorically refuse to wear skirts outside of school. I convince my mom to buy me the most masculine shoes I can find in the girls section. I am trying to be myself without telling too much. At my very Catholic school, where the nuns forbid their pupils from reading Harlequin novels or any nonlibrary books for that matter, I become brazen about my views on homosexuality. I am not afraid to tell all of my classmates that I don't think homosexual people should be pariahs in our country, that their treatment and the taunting they have endured disgusts me, most importantly that they are as human as the rest of us and should be treated as such. I am confident. I am hiding behind rhetoric, in plain sight.

Eventually, they hear me, loud and clear. There is always that person, forward enough to ask. A classmate to my left does the honor, "Est-ce que tu es lesbienne?" My heart drops so far down into my stomach I don't think it can ever get back up, yet, it propels itself back into my chest, hurts on the landing and beats faster than ever. I make a face like I am really thinking about the question. I am too cool to be offended, my hands are cold, I want her to think that I am considering her question, that right now is the only time I have ever thought about this possibility, my ears are hot, turning red with every second that passes, I think "Yes I am", but after what seems like an hour later, enunciating my answer just so she understands I mean it, I lie,

"No, I am not."

Self-preservation wins.

* * *

I am 13 years old and it is the first time in my very short life that I feel awake, emotionally and sexually. I know what it's like to be kissed by a boy, I like how it feels to be kissed, but didn't know until I met her, what really wanting to kiss another person felt like. I am moving through adolescence wanted never wanting; the day she walked in, with that backpack carelessly slung on one shoulder, I started to feel the pain of wanting without being wanted. I am lost, in her, in my desire, and most importantly in my ever-growing fear of being found out. I have to do something.

My faith in God unwavering, I pray for guidance. I am reading the bible, on my knees, fervently reciting the verses, any little chance I get, whispering Psalm 23: "The Lord is my shepherd, I lack nothing. He makes me lie down in green pastures, He leads me beside quiet waters, He refreshes my soul. He guides me along the right paths for His name's sake."

With more emphasis, I whisper it hard: "He guides me along the right paths for His name's sake." I repeat it over and over again just so he understands what I am asking him to do. I am desperate for approval. On days when I am feeling hopeful, I open my bible to the New Testament, to passages where Jesus talks of forgiveness and love, I take it in. then go lift some weights in an effort to get the biceps I have always wanted.

Other days, when everything in life seems too much for me to handle, I either spend time on the floor, sobbing, grounded by the cold weight of my father's revolver in my hand or get on myknees and read the Old Testament, which never fails to convince me that I am worthless. I go through my days waiting for God to send me a message. I want to know if there is any way He could still love me, despite my very big flaw. He never does answer. It is time for something new, I start questioning the very existence of this Father who is letting me suffer without guidance. I am ashamed and angry. Feeling abandoned, I fall deep into a depression.

Journal Entry 09/03

I am strange because I feel things forbidden to the normal members of my gender. I know that I shouldn't dwell on these feelings but I cannot help it. This person fascinates me, I love being close to her, I am afraid of touching her yet I want nothing more than to touch her. There is a certain awkwardness between us. I never know what to do when she is around. I am afraid of making sense of how I feel. I alternate between admiring her, enjoying having her close and hating her for not seeing me and my feelings.

Journal Entry 12/03

She pisses me off, she never knows anything. Can't be bothered. The only visible reaction she usually has is a weak shrug. I want to hit her, to shake her to see if that'll get a reaction. She doesn't really laugh, doesn't really get angry. I have only seen her show her feelings once. I loved when that happened because I was able to bring her out of her lethargy. She is human but too emotionally closed off. Her eyes speak volumes and I can't stop looking into them. She drives me crazy. And some days I become hopeless. With all the teenage angst and drama I can scrape together I write the words below.

Journal Entry 05/04

It is so easy to love yet so difficult to live this love. I am growing up. I am beginning to understand the situation I find myself in. I am a girl who loves another girl. I am a girl living in Haiti who loves another girl. I am a Catholic girl living in Haiti who loves another girl. I am a girl with a boyfriend I don't love who loves another girl.

Journal Entry 05/27/04

I would like to tell her how I feel but unfortunately I know that I have to keep quiet or risk losing everything that I hold dear. It would be so much easier if I loved a boy but, oh well, some things can't be changed. I am going to try to forget this period of my life because maybe if she hadn't come into my life I would have never had certain thoughts. Or maybe not. I don't know. I don't know anything anymore.

NY 2004

A few months after I turn 15 my father is murdered. At this point in my life I have already started contemplating a life of lies with a husband I sort of like and maybe even love, obediently living through infinite sessions of dull sex, imagining the resulting children who would go to Catholic schools and take dance lessons. I am making peace with that future.

That day changed everything. After many phone calls and sleepless nights, my mother has made the decision to leave our country and immigrate to New York. In the surreal territory in which my crippling grief has dragged me, I start imagining a different future. I start thinking about the friends I will make, about the other people like me who also loved in a way that wasn't acceptable, about the cargo pants and black boots I will be able to wear to school, and I begin to imagine a less lonely life.

I am at a safe distance and about to explode. I have to tell someone. I test the waters with my cousin, just trying to see if I could get myself to say the word "lesbian." I can only say "gay" because "lesbian" seems too vulgar. I say it but I don't say that I am, I don't feel like she should be the first to know. So I wait. I give it some time and when I think about it I figure out who should be the first to know.

I call her. We have the whole of the East Coast and a triangle between us. I feel safe. A calm overtakes me and I breathe out "Je suis gay." I, the confused Christian, the depressed survivor, the awkward chubby tomboy, utter the liberating word, "gay." She asks me if I had been interested in anyone back home and my heart sinks, she knows, with forced nonchalance I lie, "No, not really." A silence as long as the distance between us creeps in. We hang up. Immediately I know I should've told her the truth.

Wanting to save myself the embarrassment of having to actually say the words out loud, I decide to write her a letter. I tell her that I used to feel that way about her, I make sure she understands it was a minor thing, and that I knew that nothing could ever happen between us. I, out of fear of rejection, minimize the shit out of my feelings. I keep my closet door half closed. I am gay, but not gay and in love with my straight friend.

NY 2014

From miles away, with very little contact between us, I stayed in love. These past ten years have seen this love change shape and become a memory living alongside the heartaches and joyous moments I have accumulated throughout my journey of becoming the confident Queer masculine-of-center immigrant that I am today. I revisit this memory not only because it is an important part of my life but also because a first love deserves to be remembered, always.

-Liz Gauthier

It Happened in a Doorway

Let me recall the day I realized my masculinity.
Recognized its presence. It happened in a doorway.

It began under a tree. Covered in sweat. Under
lights and music. An awkward scene. Not yet she says.
Her hand placed almost entirely on your chest, fingers
curling slightly at the curve of your shoulders. Not a
hand to restrain. A hand to seduce. A hand placed flat,
in public, on my chest. On its tightly bound surface.

An ocean of alcohol. Nights passed on her couch.
Nights passed out between her house and mine. Nights
of almost kisses.

Days of books, classes, backs resting on lawns,
hands slightly grazing. Then a doorway.

She stands but her hands don't touch you. You
gently lean forward a sly mischievous smile, a seduction.
A close embrace, a movement of chins, a look in her eyes.

You see it, just as you lean in, a shadow, fear,
doubt, and discomfort. You see it and suddenly, there,
you are born, a man standing in front of a woman.

Consent becoming less unclear in the body this
tightly bound, in a face contorted towards masculinity

You start to think, to remember other seductions,
this body, so new, is not the one in memories.

-S Kamran

Gender and the In Between:
A GenderQueer's Journey

As a child, I spoke as few words as possible. The sound of my feminine voice disgusted me. I hated to be called a girl, while loving the color pink. I was a budding genderqueer. Boys are different from girls, they said. Fundamentally different, they'd persist. Boys don't have long hair. Boys don't like pink. Boys don't cry and boys are tough. Girls like playing with dolls. Girls do poorly at math and enjoy frilly things.

Boys. I studied them. I developed obsessions with male classmates with the utter desire to someday become all that they were. I would play make believe with my siblings in which I'd only be satisfied if I took on a male role. I connected with boys in a way I never could with girls, and never quite understood why. I would wear suspenders as a tween and feel like a boss because they would make it look like I had no chest. When I started to develop, I would wrap myself in a bandage, not realizing that was a trope practiced all too often in the trans community. I would do this until my gender identity was challenged. "You are so flat," my very influential peers would say, prompting me to ask my mother to buy me my first training bra.

And then I discovered the internet. I learned about the term transgender. I looked at hundreds upon hundreds of befores and afters, "FtMs." Top surgeries, bottom surgeries, hormones. I would read and read until my eyes would blur from my families' bright Dell desktop screen, and I'd sink in my chair, feeling the emptiness grow inside of me. It was as if the more I searched for myself, the more lost I got...because I couldn't avoid my feelings; I didn't feel fully male.

I didn't know any trans people in my anti-queer, southern town, and definitely wasn't going to be the first. So what did I do? I conformed. Like the scared child that I was, I began to present myself as outrageously feminine, so no one would suspect anything strange. It was as if I thought people could see through me, and wanted to give them no reason to use their X-ray vision to spot my insecurities...or my weirdness. I fell into a bout of shame, hating my natural femininity because I'd used a false, hyper-femininity as a wall to hide behind for so long. Oh, what a person will do to fit in. I wanted no more shame, so I turned to the bottomless internet once again, searching for a reason to love myself. I studied femininity and the power of it all. I learned that being feminine does *not* equate weakness. Femininity is powerful. It's what drives my love for community. It is the irreplaceable part of me that is capable of selfless love. In femininity, there is beauty; not the skin deep kind but the unconditional kind.

Through countless articles and books, and studying empowered feminist women like Betty Dodson and bell hooks, I learned to love my female body, and now I love it as my own. So here I am, yin and yang. Masculine and feminine. I learned to walk from male role models growing up. The color pink still makes me smile, but I feel like a lie when wearing a dress. I still bind and wear clothes from the men or boys section, and prefer to hide my curves (the little bit that I have anyway). Not because I want to look male, but because it is how I feel most comfortable.

I have little to no desire to have surgery or take hormones, though I like it when you call me "he." I don't mind "she" or "they" because I am that, too. All of the above, please. Sometimes I feel completely male, and wish on those days I had an attractive male body to wear. But most days I feel like both. I know it is confusing. I even confuse myself sometimes, but that's simply how I feel. I don't feel masculine enough to be male, nor am I feminine enough to be female. I love and accept my female body, though I ask you to not suspect that makes me a "woman."

Through my journey, I find that in terms of gender identity, you are what you say you are. A man that wears makeup and has double D's is still a man if he tells you so. It takes no more criteria than that. What it means to be a man and what it means to be a woman are social constructs, and though the masses follow these standards, you don't have to. I don't have to. I prefer to say I am in between genders, and as I feel, I am.

I spoke recently to a dear friend that had a challenging question for me. She asked:

"Why don't you just ignore gender? Why don't you just be who you are and not worry about what that makes you, be it male, female or otherwise?"

I sat there, stumped and silent, too caught off guard to admit my annoyance. I couldn't quite put my finger on it but this anger boiled inside me. I slowly felt the tingle as my senses returned and I blurted out, "Because nobody wants to be an outsider!"

I certainly didn't think before I spoke, but couldn't ignore the truth behind my words. Nobody wants to be an outsider. No one wants to feel like they belong *nowhere*. So many queer and trans people walk through their lives never feeling fully human, as if there is something alien about us that no one will ever understand. That is why we search for acceptance. That is why we challenge the gender binary and tell you to call us Zir. We're fighting for our visibility, because we don't like feeling invisible. We are human, we are present and we are all over the gender spectrum, as a gender "binary" is all but an illusion.

-Jaz Joyner

I Remember You.

Your too-tight sagging Girbaud jeans and strong taste for milkshakes spiked with too much cognac.

I remember. You.

You were not a figment of my imagination, but a distant and long forgotten memory. The nightly prayers and pillows wet with tears you gave up as offerings for a miraculous transformation did not fall on deaf ears.

You. Gentle and fun-loving boy who took care of himself with feasts of franks and beans and too much television in his young parents' absence. You who loved basketball and cabbage patch dolls equally. You were not a dream.

So when the urge to flatten your protruding chest rose back up into your heart 15 years later like a child's lost kite, you listened.

Peeled back the layers of battle wounds and arched eyebrows. Of bible verses and floor length skirts and found yourself.

Again.

You are real. The man inside of you took 33 years to become whole. To be complete from the inside out and back again.

How could I forget that we were not afraid to say what we felt? Soaking in tight embraces and all night laughter like the most porous sponge. Not yet afraid that others would see the fake selves and unspoken truths and throw it *all* away — even the real.

We are now becoming he. And instead of fractured pieces of a forgotten self we are together again.

God help anyone who dares to pull us apart. To make small what was meant to be big and full and alive. To squelch my vibrant voice into nothing but a whimper again.

I am here now. A vision in the flesh of a truth I've always known.

I Remember.

-Mekhi Baldwin

Tobacco

The last of any tobacco in my house has been smoked
Save for the cigarillo that was given to me by Ana
before I even went to the Dr
It sits on my altar as an offering, for me to remember
her, remember preciousness

I sit outside with my thoughts and palm trees' silhouette
And remember, try to at least,
That I am loved by a woman who has the capacity to hold
Everything I have in my soul is my claim
To getting better, to being not well
To dream bigger than my vices have pulled me to
extremes of not caring

I care, is the truth.
I care that I live long and well for my love
For the promise of new life, in the form of new horizons
In the form of children that are mine.

I sit with Moraga's words,
of how she mourned her child's life even while he was
alive…and still is.
I am grateful that I know her well enough to testify to life.
His.

And I am sure that if I have my own child, I will never
be free of anxiety or fear.
I wonder if the joy I might have over my own child
will be trumped by my fear of death or calamities—
from the big to the silly.
From the car crashes to the table bumps.
The constant kneading it does in my muscles.
If I will be happy with the new responsibility, this rite
of passage
Or if I will remember why I decided against children.
I hope I remember always, that the reason I thought I
could be a parent,
is because I felt confident in my co-parent.
Her.

I sit with Moraga's words,
of how she mourned her child's life even while he was
alive... and still is.
I am grateful that I know her well enough to testify to life.
His.

As for mine, I am a him, too.
I sing and there are songs about me
I can only hear when I am off stage, literally right after.
I wonder and crave to know how many more will sing
my hymns in this lifetime.
How many more will be witness, will testify to my change.

I am curious about safety, how there is none for me to
grasp ahold of.
I am reminded of spiritual texts that tell me to forget
about the day to day,
focus on the me

to remember that to be ok with groundless-ness
is to be ok with me.
And that freedom is to be unmatched by my own
notions of freedom.

I beg to differ, and yet I still maneuver around this
desire to be free of expectations

Only soon after do I recognize that I cannot
My life is not tragic, I am just not able —
I am a hymn in a him body that is read as only melody
As I strive to find rhythm in my step
To succeed the next moments.

I go back to her.
My altar of self-forgiveness.
She listens and thinks and comes back with thoughts
and pontifications, really
She thinks for me many times
I wish I knew how to do this before she comes up with
conclusions.
And I think of other hymns
Songs I sing of my thambi, of my soulbro, my sibling,
of my boys in many different cities.
I wonder if they crave safety as I do, or if they believe
that they got it
When actually, they don't.

I think of efforts to personalize our lives
The one I met in 1998 who has turned to be a beacon
of hope in the lives of so many of us who long to be sung
And I think of you, my boy, who hasn't met any of my
other hymns

And how do you know what song to sing when you are
struggling with the weight of everything.

We are female bodied.
We carry the fear of getting raped because we are
holding, still, as females do.
We push aside our needs in order to tend to other
female bodies who are fems.
We try hard to be men, or manly, while we frustratingly,
but naturally
emote as female bodies do.
And we sit and think and ponder
As masculine,
As female bodies
As butches and bois who never grow up
because holding both is never revered as a form of adult
As men who are trying to create examples of new
versions of men
who are trying to cut away to the core of this reality
As people who always need validation
In the encouraging words of our partners,
In the world's view on us being legal
Because we are trying to make sense of this world that
seemingly doesn't want us,
Definitely doesn't hold space for us.

I wonder
Why we battle
And what the new masculinity is
That remembers that we feel
That we try not to
That we want to be strong enough to hold everyone else
But us.

And I wonder
What will become of our tribe
Where will we go to get the tools,
Who will provide us with rites of passages
To ensure that
It is alright to take up space
Sometimes
Because we are
Female bodies
Our reality must be honored
Instead of being erased.
Even when we are passing as men, our realities must
be honored.
Isn't there a space that will also see us with all our
secrets and glory?
Afterall, who is better equipped with strength
to hold/stand beside
men and women.
We crave to be honored for the space we keep.
Not the space we don't.

So goodbye to girls who say we are too manlike
And goodbye to women who say we are still women
And goodbye to men who claim that they can still
have us as women
And goodbye to everyone who can't see us as whole
Who think we perform
Who don't know that we don't
Who understand gender to be two.

And hello to the beautiful people
Who help create the ceremony to honor our gifts

Hello to the women who understand that we have
something to say too,
Even when it seems like we don't.

Hello to those who love us regardless

Hello to those who respect their own complexities,
who have compassion for their layered selves, who can
therefore see us whole and without holes.

Hello to my people
Who understand
I am trying to push aside my own fears, thoughts and
inhibitions
I am trying to hold space for you too
For liberation, for freedom
It's tiring trying to be a man, when I feel things as a
woman does
It's tiring to push aside me, because the men of your
past took up so much space
It's tiring to just be, when people are asking me to
decide what I want to be, still.

Hormones or not, just say

Hello to me
Sing my hymn
Loudly
With reverence for this Divine.

Sing, so I don't have to exhale smoke
Or ingest spirit
To feel the most Godly

In me
To feel God
Around me.
Sing for me, my hymn.

-D'Lo

Mirrors/\srorriM

Outside the XY, Why Not

I am the daughter
who became the Son,
born to the mother
who became the shadow
of the father, that I would never know but dream about
often.

Walking in shoes too big to fit yet too small to take off. I
live on a tightrope of what is supposed to be and what is.
Hurting in ways never to be spoken of as I rise to the
occasion never meant for me. And then put down when I
meet the need on a human level. Needing to be different
and being different blurs the lines of my reality,

I break   and
rebuild

seamlessly.

I am the sister outsider who walks as the brother inside
only catching glimpses of my true self in overpriced,
broken mirrors.

I am
living in imposed realities with set agendas of entities
that only want to see me fail, setting bail on the existence
of life cuz somehow it affects you that I have a wife.

They hate me, so in places hard to admit, I hate
myself, but I'm good at disguising it with consumer
love. Lost in a world of so-called community, I
decipher the under tones and translate it into
communing with me.

Who I am¬
who I would like to be
are sometimes mutually exclusive.

I have been excluded out of the XY. As you look into to
my eyes and tell me lies I take a deep breath. It is not
enough.

A piece of the pie can't suffice. The hunger I feel is
my will to be free and it lives long after me.

For my legacy,

I am able to breathe in pain and exhale love and my roots
run deeper than the tallest oak

cuz even when I'm broke, I'm still rich with the things
that money could never buy.

I am strong with that native pride.

Seeing me--for real evens the deal of a crooked deck. I
don't need validation that

I
am
a
man

because eyes go blind with grains of sand polluting
them over time with hate.

So I work while I wait.

see,
me and freedom will find each other one day, even if it
means being free from the x.
x, x, of the Y, cuz see being and flying without wings
is no easy task so here is my first confession; I am
ripping off the mask.

I am the warrior who carries the message no matter the
weight.

-Chino Hardin

A Whisper

A whisper, just one, sent her reeling, "you're just not man enough," is what she heard. She loved everything about her but needed that.

Thirty-eight years into life and this was a first. Being a lesbian had meant many different things over the years but "not being man enough" wasn't ever really a concern. The idea was to be yourself, to love yourself and transform beyond what you had been told your entire life. But here you were, armor clad and well worn, defending yourself against a known but now unknown assailant.

You had fallen, she had fallen and that had been enough for you. You changed your underwear, your bras, there were no bows, ribbons or pink. There was no "lady" about you except for your heart, your emotion, and your sensitivity if those are lady things.

Crying and open, you found yourself exposed. Years of work spent exfoliating the stuff of your heart was now backfiring. Your emotional freedom and boundary-less living just wasn't sexy. The openness was in fact an abyss to her, something to be wary of, something to fill, erase, and ignore. But that is work that is never done, undone, cannot be so.

You stand mirror entranced, examining the face you've known. Could you be someone else? Something more? Un-tap a part chained?

The answer comes quickly, a resounding no, a mask perhaps but not the core.

A list of good things about yourself: recite, repeat, recite, repeat. You are ok as you are ladyboy, boygul, soft butch, too pretty to be a _____.

Broken, cracked sits your sense of self. How can you love now knowing that your expression is simply not good enough?

Hung but not hung.

To add something that was never there or needed, feels like the true death.

A list of one to 10; you are ranked. Weighing the odds of happiness and despair. You deem yourself too heavy for all of that.

Waves crash. Darkness is complete. You close your eyes but see only repetition.

I am not this because you are not that.

Lack clouded devotion, clouding not basic love but lust.

She sleeps sound in her release.

You dream of water, frozen and crashing in on you exposing you to the elements. You think that you will die in this dream blizzard and cry out for help because this is what you have been taught to do.

Children, snot nosed and toe headed, wake you.

-Robin Cloud

Body: Heart and Mind

The Mind

A long journey of self-discovery, exploration and affirmation of my boihood has brought me to this point in my life. From the time of my childhood, I felt the influence of my preferred gender expression¬along with its consequences. It was mysterious to me that the importance of frills and "feminine" behavior outweighed the feelings that I actually had towards what I wanted to do. Being excommunicated by half my family when I came out at the age of 15 taught me that who I am and what is imposed on me will be a conflict that I encounter for the rest of life. This is common sentiment amongst those who are not under the umbrella of hetero-normativity, but the internal battle between my sex and gender identity was a crisis that I did not find much support for. The curvy lumps on my chest made my face burn at every examination in the mirror. I felt like I was in the middle of an ambiguous place, welcoming of my biological sex but incredibly frustrated by the breasts that interfered with my masculine expression.

Today, explaining my fluidity of my identity is still a challenge that I face, but I have become comfortable in vocalizing LGBTQ concerns as a student activist and educator. I share my story and experiences, but also advocate for human rights through youth outreach, events on my college campus and work with LGBTQ organizations. This active role that I have taken in my life has encouraged me to think beyond the confines of what society and my own body have afforded me. I have come to terms with my physical body as a half-complete representation of myself, but I have also learned that settling is not the way to achieve self and outward acceptance. This surgery is a turning point in my journey because my physical changes will be a concrete symbol of the challenges, learning and self-love that I've experienced. I will be empowered by the outward expression of an identity I have felt my whole life, and that opportunity is invaluable to me.

Many people view top surgery as a transformative experience from which a new person emerges. While top surgery will impact my life tremendously, I do not view the procedure as a transformation at all. As a gender non-conforming biological woman, I acknowledge the experience of living a sexual and gender duality. I recognize the capabilities and limitations that my body has in terms of encompassing all of my gender identity. For me, that means embracing the combination of comfort with my sexual anatomy, but discomfort with the breasts that take away from the masculine aesthetic that I express. The physical change that I intend to undergo will not alter the person I have been, but it will close the gap between what I experience internally and how that is reflected in my physique. What I look forward to most about the outcome of this is wholly experiencing myself in the mirror of my self-reflection.

This surgery is not a step for me, but rather the full

necessary change that will make me comfortable in my skin and mind. I feel that my surgery is important because it is a representation of the broad spectrum that the word "transgender" refers to; the fact that I am not a female-to-male transgender individual does not take away from the physical anxiety I feel within a body that does not encompass my personal identity. I am proud to push the boundaries of gender by being a non-conforming person, and I will be even more proud to bear that limitlessness in my physicality.

The Heart

I carried you. I was told to make you. I did make you. I did not make you. You carried me for 21.5 years. I was your definition. Your label. Their sign. I hurt you. I pained you.

I am sorry. It took me so long to understand. Forgive me. I did not know better. I was written into life in its very beginning. I was told to make you.

I never made you.

You carried me. There was no consent. I hurt you. I pained you. Forgive me. I was not you. I am not you.

I was never your label. Never their sign. You dismantled me. I am not your master.

Now you thrive.

-Renee Vallejo

for all of us

For all the trans folks
shut out
of communities they helped build,
poured lifeblood into,
fueled movements that thrive on love
for justice;
shut out
of communities that complain
of intolerance from without,
but take within
the same hypocritical stances of
"just us" mentalities,
forgetting that we all be bound
by lies that seek to strip us of our
humanity,
separate our bodies from our selves,
create new roles that are alien to our souls
For all the trans fags
discarded
by men who fantasize gym-toned masculinities
packaged in prototypes and
HRC-fed dreams of happily ever after
that never heal the brokenness of

bklyn boihood

internalized homophobia,
externalized:
"no fats, no femmes, no fags";
discarded
by men who mar their sexualities
with their fear of our bodies,
invade them with presumption,
reduce them to enigmas
lacking a
satisfying
delicious
throbbing
rock
hard
cock
For all the bois of darker hues,
bridged by
loss and light
to ancestors whose bodies were also brutalized
by terror,
ruling class greed that meant to choke
love and life
from mass incarcerated conduits;
bois whose hearts
beat against the unhearing
ears of those encamped behind walls of silence
that will not protect
our voices sing
powerful truths,
of brown queer masculinities:
beautiful in their intersections,
resonant in their reprising.
we have always been here,

precious
and
worthy of loving.

-Melvin Whitehead

To the College Bois

This is a letter for the college bois. For the bois who feel invisible. For the bois on the yard. For the bois who are wondering, is it just me?

First, you're not alone. I know it's not easy walking around a campus or even finding access to classes online, and no one looks like you. Your feelings of isolation are valid. These institutions were never made for us. However, let it be known, that these institutions were built by us. Our blood lives in the land, stone, and brick of these buildings. Your ancestry is one of kings, queens, rulers, and knowledge generators. So, these two realities live in contradiction to one another. No one may say it to you, but you belong there. There is a seat for you at the table.

However, let's talk about the table. I'm sure applying to a college or university was a process in itself. From the moment you started to fill out the application, questions about gender, sex, race, economic status permeated from the page. Perhaps these things felt odd for you to fill out. But, trust, every question had a purpose. You are asked from the moment of applying, who are you? So, I ask you now to consider, who are you…really? No amount of check marks or fill in-the-blank options can reveal your value to this world. So, who are you currently and who do you want to become?

One thing I learned about the college experience is that if you set the intentions, you can control the outcomes. You've been invited to a table and sometimes that table will be adorned with limitless amounts of resources, campus cultural terms, and ways of being. Yet, you may also be invited to a table and not given the proper utensils to enjoy the meal. You may have to ask to be fed. You may have to question the lack of service provided. Find your voice. Activate and interrogate. Ask questions. Listen to your environment but most importantly, listen to yourself. Listen to your body. It's full of knowledge. It's your database. Trust your instincts and find your resources.

Once you've been admitted to a college or university, know your resources. You'll receive tons of information about programmatic and resource offerings. It is important for you to find those recourses. Sustainability practices around care are essential. So, I urge you to think about your wellness. Who do you need in your circle for survival? Some of these resources might reflect the multiplicity of your cultural or gender identities. Yet, some of these resources are hidden. There will be people and allied communities who will want to support you. Let them. You will learn to resource yourself. You will learn about accessing the multiple truths around resilience. You've prevailed before and you will prevail again. This process might feel uncomfortable. But, the growth is in the discomfort.

Each year, you will learn more about yourself, the

field or specialty you decide to study, and the institution you've decided to join. You are an expert regarding your lived experience. Your truth will grow as you learn about the many truths of the world. There will be times that you may want to walk away from this experience. That's alright. I do not think college is for everyone and I think we each have our own path to greatness. There isn't a wrong or a right way to explore your educational goals. You may need to hit "pause" and come back to it. Colleges and universities aren't going anywhere, so you can always come back, if that's what you want. I ask, what do you want? This is a broad question but putting yourself at the center of this experience is necessary. The college experience is about YOU.

To the college bois, this letter is for you. You matter to me and I see you. If no else sees you, I do. From the moment I stepped onto the yard, I knew I was different. I knew that people weren't used to my complexities. I changed my major a few times and I found my passion. I knew I wanted to work in college environments. There's money out there for us to transform systems. There's professional training and programs that are free. If you want to work for a college, you can and there's a place for you here. We need you. I need you. And if you need me, I'm here.

College will provide you with lots of knowledge but don't forget there are always multiple truths, so don't be afraid to continue to generate new knowledge. Information is always out there but the access isn't always visible. Search for it, ask questions, and seek answers. But, do not neglect yourself. Love yourself, fiercely. Never forget about self-love. Form networks of love around you so you don't slip between the cracks of invisibility. Relationships are powerful and necessary. What you know is important but WHO you know is critical. Who builds you up? Who keeps you connected? Who keeps you grounded? I encourage you to keep a love journal. Write letters to yourself and keep a list of people who support you, unconditionally. You need them...just like they need you.

Lastly, to the college bois, I love you. I love you for all of your resilience. I love you for your efforts. I love you for your brilliance. You keep me going. So, when someone asks me, why do I continue to show up to work, I reply... "for the bois..." Thank you, for all that you are and will continue to be.

With love,

Dr. Van Bailey
Inagural Director, LGBTQ Center, University of Miami
Inaugural Director, BGLTQ Student Life, Harvard College
Denison Class of 2005, the Ohio State University Class of 2007, CSU-Northridge Class of 2012

Boi

New Orleans
Black in the middle of spring
Brass players congregating
As we prepare for the second line
My gown covering internal agony
What's next?
Success, failure, endless possibilities
Love covering my skin
Sweat drenching from my locs
Grass beneath my feet
I walk in violation
The leaders of the elite institution said:
All women must wear black dresses to commencement
No professor ever gave a lesson on gender expression
Why must womanhood be wrapped in expectation?
So I wear black
Black button, slacks and loafers
All designed for male
Partially following directions
But why must I be directed by gender
I've always fallen somewhere in between
Restroom doors swinging off of filthy hinges
With signs dangling

Reading male or female
There is no third entrance
The world gender phobic
I gender fucked
Piss runs down my leg in disbelief
Who knew that dumping waste could be so complicated?
I was taught to act like a lady
Institutionalized to be feminine
Somewhere in between learning to put on lip gloss
I feel in love with masculinity
Hiding my body from the hyper sexual fantasies of men twice my age
Joe boxers painting against these curvy hips
Like graffiti paints a glow on cold brick in Los Angeles
I hid myself behind graphic tees that said: Fuck you pay me
Pay me attention
It's take a lot courage to be vulnerable
Walking in violence
Men afraid of losing privilege
Women afraid of difference
Dapper, clean cut
Locs twisted to the scalp
Tappers, line of precision
See I make masculinity look pretty
We make masculinity look pretty
Me&MyBois
Brooklyn Boi
Brown Boi
Theta Boi
Queer Boi
Boi
B-O-I

Born obviously incredible
Wear that bowtie with pride
Folded into perspective
Difference is not taught but learn to be subordinate
In elementary school
Perspective felt meaningless
Abnormality fractured faces on the playground
Potential was written on the wall with chalk
I was a masterpiece easily erased
Blood covering skin
Knuckles tearing my beauty
Feet folding and stomping my insides out
Bullied for being a he she
I guess they thought they could beat the man out of me
Who am I safe to be?
Resiliency made me a success
I am BOI
B-O-I
Beaten outwardly and internally
Difference holds so much potential
Boi
Born obviously incredible
Especially when you wear it pretty.

-Megan Benton (aka Emotions the Poet)

Masculine of Centre, Seeks Her Refined Femme

In this essay, I explore female masculinities of colour that lie outside of the iconic butch narrative, i.e., womyn[1] like me. I stumbled into academia quite by accident. I cut my teeth on political campaigns and worked with social justice organizations around the country. I'd always felt that the conversations that take place in academic spaces lacked roots in the communities I come from and live in. Sure, there was never a shortage of stories about these places that I call home, but the real stories, told by people who look like me, have more often been told through personal narrative, film, and art. When I found myself sitting in the Gender Institute at the London School of Economics, I struggled with the absence of stories about people like me—queer womyn of colour along a masculine continuum whose lives and loves don't get told, who have to search for reflections of our stories in the margins of butch narratives, the constant sidekicks and stereotyped footnotes of "minority masculinity."

So I set out on a quest that has led me all the way to this book in your hands. I had some amazing conversations along the way. When I set out to write, I realized that I didn't even have the language I needed to reach out to my community, though I'd long known what butch meant, thanks to my butch elders. Even though I called myself butch, all around me there were signals about what that was supposed to look like, and the word never fully reflected who I am. One of my first conversations with Oshen T., an activist and she-pronoun-using stud, echoed this un-ease with which many of us take up the mantle of butch.

> "I identify as stud but, growing up, I didn't know that there was a word, "stud." What was more common was butch, but at some point, like in my mid to late teens, I noticed that butches were usually white women, and even though I did see some black butches... at some point it got really irritating and didn't fit me. I don't feel butch, and I don't like that word, even saying it. Stud came out of me and my peers having a conversation, and I held onto the word stud. We younger studs from East Oakland started to gravitate toward that. Butch was white and older, and as young kids, we were studs. There was some age stuff, race and class. All the books were about stone cold butches... just white people. We were like, nah, that's not us."
> —Oshen T.

If butch wasn't the word I was looking for, what was it? Should I use dom? Stud? AG (aggressive)? None of these quite worked, and so in 2008 I introduced the term "masculine of centre" (MoC) as more encompassing and less racially and class- specific than butch. MoC also speaks to the cultural nuances of female masculinity, while still recognizing our commonalities—independent of who we partner with. The inclusion of the language "of centre" sees beyond the traditional binary of male and female to female masculinity as a continuum. "Of centre" is a way of acknowledging that the balance each of us determines around our own masculinity and femininity in the discovery of our gendered selves is never truly fixed. Masculine of centre recognizes the cultural breadth and depth of identity for lesbian/queer womyn who tilt toward the masculine side of the gender scale, and the term includes a wide range of identities such as butch, stud, aggressive/AG, tom, macha, boi, dom, etc.

Over the last two decades, queer gender theory, influenced by Judith Butler's discourse on gender performativity[2] has evolved to incorporate analysis of butch gender and female masculinity.[3] This analysis has produced a range of understandings regarding the social construction of butch consciousness, female masculinity, and sexual expression and identity. The argument suggests that every individual constructs a personal narrative that reflects their gendered self. As these theoretical frameworks around "butch" emerge as areas for critical inquiry and awareness, so do questions addressing their limitations.

Existing work on female masculinity and butch identity has crossed numerous disciplines such as queer theory, masculinity studies, psychology, and ethnic studies. Butch themes have emerged from beyond the academy into poetry, film, biography and autobiography, and fiction. Yet, despite this explosion of work, including the emergence of female masculinity as a theoretical concept, theorizations of "butchness" among womyn of colour are largely absent from the academic canon on gender. Even as authors such as Sherrie Inness in "'G. I. Joes in Barbie Land': Recontextualizing Butch in Twentieth-Century Lesbian Culture" and S. Bear Bergman in Butch is a Noun have disrupt- ed the "fixed" understandings of "butch gender" in the master narrative, very little of this work has challenged its construction as a racialized identity.

I think it's possible to tell this story, my story, without chang- ing the rich history and stories of how the mainstream butch narrative has created the social and political space we all live in, and which makes it possible to write this piece. The deep irony is that historically butch identities have been more embraced among MoC womyn of colour than by white queer com- munities. Despite this rich history and legacy, the image of what butch looks like in popular media and academic writing is still overwhelmingly white. I want to begin creating room within the existing narrative for young womyn of colour to explore the in- tersections of our gender and race as critical sites that inform our identity. It is in that spirit that I offer "masculine of centre" as a space to unify all of our vibrant transformative, feminist, gender queer ways of knowing so that we can build social and political power together.

Raging Bulls: Icons of a White Female Masculinity

Theorists[4] have explored what some have called "lesbian gender" in its many forms, including butch identity, femme identity, and female masculinity. This theorizing has not only validated the lives of masculine-of-centre womyn, but has also been instrumental in framing butch as a construction of gendered identity, rather than as a "role." The construction of butch and its ability to be read requires that certain representations come to reflect its essence as an identity. Such representations have in the past been referred to as "classic" or "classical."[5] The contemporary establishment of a "butch aesthetic," has, by producing representations of itself, "effectively refused the multiplicity of cultural, social, and political intersections in which the concrete array"[6] of butch identity is actually constructed.

While focusing on demonstrating butch and female masculinity's epistemological origins, many feminist theorists have interpreted butch as a way of "knowing, interpreting, and doing lesbian gender." Ontologically, these lesbian genders are seen as being "concerned with having an identity, and a kind of true self."[7] Some understand it as both socially constructed "gender performance" and others as representing an essentialized heterosexual, biological, male identity that merely clones the referent. The expressions of one's gendered butch identity are intrinsically linked to culture and race. In Davis and Kennedy's classic

Boots of Leather, Slippers of Gold: The History of a Lesbian Community, they describe "a new style of butch, a woman who dressed in working-class male clothes for as much of the time as she possibly could, and went to the bar every day, not just on weekends. She was also street wise and fought back physically when provoked by straight society or by other lesbians."[8] The political significance of this emergence lies in the visibility lesbians gained in the 1940s and '50s as World War II reshaped the American landscape, changing women's roles in relationship to work, gender, and family. Butch was a site of resistance to the heteronormative limitations on women. It was a place to embrace one's identity in a public way that allowed for alignment between the public and private self, a way of claiming space with your very presence.

There is a long-standing history of butch representations that have helped solidify the iconic image of today's butch. The icon of butch identity was fashioned through historical narratives, poetry, biography, and classic novels such as Radclyffe Hall's The Well of Loneliness, written in 1928 and long considered the most well-known lesbian novel, The Beebo Brinker Chronicles from Ann Bannon, which moved butch into mainstream consciousness in the 1950s, and Leslie Feinberg's Stone Butch Blues, set in the pre-Stonewall era of the 1960s, which solidified the archetype. This "butch raging bull," as Halberstam argues,[9] is meant to "offer masculinity a new champion" drawing on the iconography of the white male boxer.

These works created a narrative for what and how butch looks and feels that still holds significant cultural power today. The external signifiers—the class and racial location of these historical accounts and cultural references to bars and customs—locate butch identity. This locating of butchness within a specific culture, class, race, and ethnicity makes it difficult for the masculine of centre person of colour to enter into the narrative without their gender presentation, specifically their version of masculinity, being questioned.

Attempts to disrupt this sense of "classical" butch

continue to rely on representations and cultural location within whiteness and white notions of masculinity and femininity. As Halberstam points out, there is cultural value in marginalizing masculinities that divert from the master narrative.[10] Even though Halberstam is speaking to heteronormative masculinity here, these divert- ing narratives have the potential to "dilute" the "authoritative power" of white butchness in the same way. As this narrative is pushed into the mainstream queer consciousness to construct butch identity, many of our experiences are left out. Supporting versions of masculinity that we enjoy and trust, many of these "heroic masculinities" depend absolutely on the— subordination of alternative masculinities.[11] This role of the dominant narrative being constructed and circulated while simultaneously preventing alternative narratives is an important factor in establishing fixed understandings of female masculinity and butch.

Halberstam[12] goes on to address female masculinity's relation to whiteness and identifies it as a site of inquiry for "cultural studies" yet does not venture down the road of how the relationship to race critically alters female masculinity as a concept. The challenge in theorizing butch gender and identity is that to deter- mine how it operates, you have to locate it within certain bodies and cultural and sexual practices. These various locations, when analyzed, become fixed and static through the work of the writer exploring their creation and development. A central argument in Female Masculinity is that masculinity "becomes legible as masculinity where and when it leaves the white male middle-class body."[13] While a considerable amount of the analysis explores when and where the narrative departs from the male body, less attention is given to when and where it departs from whiteness.

Unlike white female masculinity, female masculinity for womyn of colour is based on sites of power and systemic oppression— through masculinities of colour. The assumption that they can be resignified with equal subversive and revolutionary actions against white manhood is false. The ability to access masculinity pivots upon the ways in which gender intersects with race, and these gaps have been filled with many new ways of naming ourselves. In the last decade, the explosion of young masculine-of-centre womyn has created a demographic shift on the butch landscape, giving way to terms like "stud," "boi," "tom," and "macha" in California and the South, "dom" within the DC, Maryland, and Virginia region, and "aggressives," or "AGs" in New York.

These identities represent a redefined female masculinity that is rooted in the experiences of womyn of colour and is more gen- derqueer than historical interpretations of butch. For some this raises the question: "What is happening to all of our butches?" I think this evolution highlights the fact that, for many of us who came of age ten or twenty years ago, and even called ourselves butches, we never felt fully rooted in that language and space. As a community, we have the opportunity to respond with an open heart to this evolution, ensuring that the legacy of butch as a so- cial, political, and personal space continues to grow and thrive. But we must also concede its limitations. The title of this piece, "Masculine of Centre, Seeks Her Refined Femme," is a heading from the first dating profile posted using the term "masculine of centre." It speaks to both a historical legacy of butch-femme and a longing for a language different and new.

Masculine of centre is already moving into mainstream consciousness in queer spaces, white as well as of colour. Organizations such as BUTCH Voices, whose mission is to enhance and sustain the well-being of all women, female-bodied, and trans- identified individuals who are masculine of centre, and online communities such as thedefinition.org (for masculine-of-centre women, transmen, and our allies) have integrated masculine of centre into their mission statements as a broader calling to our communities.

The emergence of this new language would not have happened were it not for the ways in which masculine-of-centre womyn of colour live their female masculinity through the lens of race. Our identity has socially transformative powers and there are still nuances to our identities—masculine-of-centre mothering, social mobility, and historical racial oppression—which shape masculinity in ways that have yet to be fully explored. What masculine-of-centre womyn of colour do with masculinity, how we interpret it, and how we embody it, contains lessons for other womyn and men, both queer and straight, regardless of race.

This is an invitation for all of us to reshape female masculinity through our experiences so that we may better understand the whole of who we are.

Notes

[1] Womyn here is used to reflect that, for many of us, as masculine of centre, our gendered identity is not accurately reflected in the term women.

[2] See the Sources list at the end of this essay.

[3] Sue Ellen Case, "Toward a Butch Femme Aesthetic," in The Lesbian and Gay Studies Reader, eds. Henry Ablelove, Michella Aina Barale, and David M. Alperin (New York; London: Routledge, 1993), 295–306; Judith Halberstam, Female Masculinity (Durham, NC: Duke University Press, 1998); Sally R. Munt, Butch/Femme: Inside Lesbian Gender (Washington: Cassell, 1998); Heidi M. Levitt and Sharon G. Horne, "Exploration of Lesbian-Queer Genders: Butch, Femme, Androgynous or 'Other'" Journal of Lesbian Studies 6 (2002), 25–39.

[4] Case, in The Lesbian and Gay Studies Reader, 37; Joan Nestle, The Persistent Desire: A Femme-Butch Reader (Boston: Alyson Publications, 1992); Madeline D. Davis and Elizabeth Lapovsky Kennedy, Boots of Leather, Slippers of Gold: The History of a Lesbian Community (New York; London: Routledge, 1993); Halberstam, Female Masculinity; Munt, Butch/Femme.

[5] Case, 37.

[6] Judith Butler, Gender Trouble: Feminism and the Subversion of Iden- tity (New York; London: Routledge, 1990), 83.

[7] Munt, Butch/Femme, 1.

[8] Davis and Kennedy, Boots of Leather, Slippers of Gold, 68.

[9] Halberstam, Female Masculinity, 43. 10   ibid, 1.

[11-13] ibid.

Sources

Ardill, Susan and Sue O'Sullivan. "Butch/Femme Obsessions," Femi- nist Review 34 (1990): 79–85.

Bannon, Ann. The Beebo Brinker Chronicles. New York: Triangle Classics-Quality Paperback Book Club, 1995.

Bergman, S. Bear. Butch Is a Noun. Vancouver: Arsenal Pulp Press, 2010.

Butler, Judith. "Merely Cultural," Social Text: Queer Transexions on Race, Nation, and Gender 52/53 (1997): 265–77.

———. Gender Trouble: Feminism and the Subversion of Identity. New York: Routledge. 1999.

Case, Sue Ellen, "Toward a Butch Femme Aesthetic." In The Lesbian and Gay Studies Reader edited by Henry Ablelove, Michelle Aina Barale, and David M. Halperin, 295–306. New York; London: Rout- ledge, 1993.

Davis, Madeline D. and Elizabeth Lapovsky Kennedy. Boots of Leather, Slippers of Gold: The History of a Lesbian Community. New York; London: Routledge, 1993.

Feinberg, Leslie. Stone Butch Blues: A Novel. New York: Firebrand Books, 1993.

Halberstam, Judith. "Mackdaddy, Superfly, Rapper: Gender, Race, and Masculinity in the Drag King Scene." Social Text: Queer Transexions on Race, Nation, and Gender 52/53 (1997): 104–31.

———. Female Masculinity. Durham, NC: Duke University Press, 1998.

Hall, Radclyffe. The Well of Loneliness. New York: Anchor Books, 1990.

Inness, Sherrie and Michele Lloyd. "'G. I. Joes in Barbie Land': Recontextualizing Butch in Twentieth-Century Lesbian Culture." NWSA Journal 7 no. 3 (1995): 1–23.

136 • PERSISTENCE

Levitt, Heidi M. and Sharon G. Horne. "Exploration of Lesbian-Queer Genders: Butch, Femme, Androgynous or 'Other.'" Journal of Les- bian Studies 6 (2002): 25–39.

Levitt, Heidi M. and Katherine R. Hiestand, "A Quest for Authenticity: Contemporary Butch Gender." Sex Roles 50 no. 9–10 (2004): 605–21.

Munt, Sally R. Butch/Femme: Inside Lesbian Gender. Washington: Cassell, 1998.

Nestle, Joan. "Butch-Fem Relationships: Sexual Courage in the 1950s." Heresies 12 no. 22 (1981): 21–24

———. A Restricted Country. New York: Firebrand Books, 1987.

———. The Persistent Desire: A Femme-Butch Reader. Boston: Alyson

Books, 1992.

Oshen T., Interview with author. Oakland, CA. September 1, 2010. Phelan, Shane. "Public Discourse and the Closeting of Butch Lesbians." In Butch/Femme: Inside Lesbian Gender, edited by Sally R.

Munt, 191–99. Washington: Cassell, 1998.

Walidah, Hanifah and Olive Demetrius. U People, DVD. UPeople LLC, 2007. www.iLoveUPeople.com

-B. Cole

Homebois Don't Write Enough

For Ignacio Rivera, Kit Yan, Aemilius Ramirez, Ryan-Li Dahlstrom, & Cris Izaguirre

homebois we don't write enough love poems.
we rename ourselves izzie from Isabella,
casey from Cassandra, kay from Kathleen.
we run out of ink for our stories cuz we've been
running through doors of male and female, never
satisfied.
we stuntin' baggy jeans and bright colors over the sirens,
we stop cars and walk with stride that makes the
concrete self-conscious
about its own stability.
hitting pavement at the tiptoes of summer,
there you go talkin' about how you
"need a woman pregnant and barefoot."
as I shutter asking,
are you gonna find a stiletto ready to stab you
if the nightsticks don't come get you first?
asking- are you gonna be that bullet that is a mouth?
asking- are you gonna be that missile that blasts your
love until
she/he/zie/they miss you,

even when you will both be in the same bed?
if we make ourselves harder than bone,
make us a legacy that is beyond all this.
cuz I've been running through doors of male and female,
never satisfied.
that makes you nervous doesn't it?
are you worried, your palms sweaty
because I am NOT that kind of a man
AG
stud
butch
boi
warrior
comrade
man
and that might make you obsolete, that means this
whole system
needs a revision. that means, we have to ask ourselves
daily
are you are doing your homework?
homebois, we don't write enough love poems to
ourselves.
spell out our soft syllables unapologetically, letting
the ferocity in us extend us a strength beyond stiff jaw
and cold silence,
the stuff of abandoned buildings.
let us unfold the photos with us dipped in lace and
dresses and embrace them, laugh.
let the most tender cipher surround us not be our
mother's tears for the loss
of a daughter.
let us hold our breaths for the sakia gunn's and the
fong lees, as it

could easily be our sweat on this sidewalk.
let us adore the swiftness of kisses in moonlight rather than the
pummeling cusses of strangers scared of difference.
let the tensile ace bandage be a testament across this chest, waving like prophets
of a gender war.
let every poor, black, brown, yellow & mixed race butch see her way into a paintbrush,
a camera, an uprock, a computer, and not into the hips of hand grenades chucked on someone else's homeland.
to every person who squirms in the bathrooms, classrooms, bus stops.
and on stages next to me,
let them know that this moment is a clue of your queerness.
let them know my titas are at casinos burning this American dream away too.
let them know my kuyas christen their kid's foreheads and give me daps with the same hands.
let them know that each time they make fun of us, they could be in a feather boa,
singing prince, showing their wives some force that will drive them toward and not away.
let their children run up and down the city
as the confident queer kids, who get
you being the backward parent they divulge to teachers they are ashamed of.
scholarships to college for a GSA or for the protests & poems they manifest,
let me not reveal my monster each time I hear
"I'll fuck you straight."
let my fingers not be readied trigger,

grabbing sharp objects for stabbing back, to turn them into
the bloodiest meat they make of me with their pyramid of power.
let me walk away
without harm,
disbanding my razor-edge that could cut their lifelines,
slice steel song into their temples,
shear off their pride as soon as they start to unzip their pants.
let us know we can do this
and make it clear:
We choose not to.
if we can make ourselves harder than bone,
if we can make ourselves harder than stone,
make us a legacy that is beyond all this.

-Kay Ulanday Barrett

Women Who Dare to Be Themselves: The Creation of The Jerry Palmer Group of Detroit

Spaces for women of color living on multiple marginal intersections are sacred and rare. That's why I found it worth my time to share my excitement about the new grassroots organization we started in Detroit in August of this year, The Jerry Palmer Group. It was in 2011 when the ALORDE Collective, a Black lesbian health group, held an herstoric gathering at my home that brought together three generations of Black lesbians. Alexis Gumbs and Julia Wallace from Mobile Homecoming, facilitated and filmed the event. During the conversation, it was suggested that those of us 30 and over who are masculine-identified, outreach to those in the younger generation by having a support group at the Ruth Ellis Center (an agency that serves homeless LGBTQ youth). However, no one followed through on this brilliant idea even though there were individuals who said they wanted to be involved. So needless to say, the idea laid dormant for some time.

One day, out of nowhere, I get a phone call from a fellow community member asking for help. A friend of his, who is a high school principal, contacted him with a sense of urgency. According to the school principal, a large number of teenage girls had been acting out in extremely aggressive ways. When I spoke to the principal, she shared that these behaviors included the formation of a gang. Not surprisingly, the principal was told by staff that many of these girls were "forcing" other girls to "become lesbian." Right way, I knew that these girls were getting into lots of trouble at school and that the school staff were clueless about what to do and how to accurately describe what they were seeing. In addition, I listened as the principal identified these students as masculine in appearance. As she spoke, I began to think about the group that was supposed to start a support group for masculine-identified lesbian (MIL) youth. It occurred to me that this must be the right time to revisit this idea, but this school is in crisis at the moment and in need of some immediate help. That's when I contacted 12 MIL's that I knew of who I could count on and who would be interested, and also had some experience with youth. I asked them if they would commit to one full year of being a mentor and to forming an organization that could address these and similar issues as they arise. It was becoming apparent that women like us (MILs) were needed in the community and that we have an opportunity to serve in ways that others can't.

I was reminded of groups that had already existed such as Brown Bois, Bklyn Boihood, New Millennium Butches, the Butch Voices conference, and the Unity Fellowship Church MIL Ministry. I had also conducted safe space workshops for Black MIL's for some years now, and knew the value of butch bonding and self-empowerment. But I also knew that young MIL's in Detroit weren't being exposed to older MIL's, mainly because the older generation had not done all we could to connect with the youth by being visible and spending quality time. I say this because I'm over 50 myself and belong to the older generation. We forget that when we first came out as a lesbian, there were older MIL's that were role models for us. One of them was Jerry Palmer.

Jerry Palmer was old enough to be my parent. Her presence made me strong. Jerry looked like a Black man and she was typically mistaken as one. She was a woman who was very masculine and never made apologies for it. Her existence allowed me to be all of who I am. She passed away at the age of 86 in 2012. Jerry's courage to be herself back in a time long before there was more acceptance for a minority attractional orientation and gender expression, inspired the name for this group. It was also a way of honoring all those butches, studs, jaspers, and dykes of color whose names never got into any LGBT history book but who were courageous enough to live out their truth with pride in an era when it was risky to do so.

It was clear to us, the leadership cadre of the Jerry Palmer Group, that we wanted to assist the staff school by reaching out to these students and making ourselves available for guidance, support, and as a resource for them. Having worked with youth before, we were aware of how important it is to establish a trusting relationship with the students and be willing to show up for them, consistently. We also realize what a difference it makes to connect with someone who looks like us, especially when we belong to a minority group such as this. Positive roles models are hard to find, and our group made the decision to step up and take responsibility for being visible and accessible for the youth. At the same time, we anticipate that the youth have a lot to offer to us in terms of their knowledge and insights.

This "wake up call" for us motivated our group to develop broad goals that would extend throughout the entire Detroit community. My fellow JPG leaders agree to the mission for the organization: To combine the talents of self-identified masculine lesbians (MILs) into a cohesive effort to give validation, support and resources to MILs of all ages in the Detroit metropolitan area, as well as across the country where such support is needed. This grassroots self-reliant group specializes in educating the public about the social and cultural experiences of African American MILs and others of color because this is a population often neglected, devalued, and rarely highlighted in national discussions about the LGBT community. Since this is a self-help peer support organization, MILs serve as leaders in proactively managing the programs of this collective group. The JPG strives to collaborate and partner with similar groups such as Brooklyn Boihood, Brown Boi Project, Unity Fellowship Church Movement MIL Ministry, and Butch Voices to encourage participation in the intersected social justice movements where women of color are marginalized and disempowered.

We agreed to focus on a five-point platform consisting of Self Education, Education to the Public, Support Group, Consultation, and Activities/Outreach.

The Self Education component is our way of

ensuring attention paid to building insights into ourselves, our various identities, our bodies, our health, our oppression, our privileges, our strengths, our challenges, our relationships with our families, and how we treat each other as Black MILs and MILs in general. We help each other with coping strategies for dealing with the daily micro-aggressions (insults) and do some noncompetitive bonding. We owe it to ourselves redefine ourselves, and to celebrate the diversity within the spectrum of Black MILs while learning how to take care of ourselves.

Education to the Public is our way of saying that we don't expect everyone to know what an MIL is and how to appropriately address us when they encounter us. It's up to us as MILs to provide some level of information as a way of enlightening folks to our experiences in the world. It's through this process that empathy towards our humanity is developed, a path toward social justice. For example, teaching the concept of Gender Expression, may help others understand why many MILs refuse to be called "ma'am" and "lady."

The Support Group component is the program that brings MILs together in safe spaces for the self-help and building of mutual respect and trust. Above all, we are geared toward connecting the generations and making a way for promoting healthy dialogues, mutual guidance, direction, and ways to navigate the dilemmas that often occur when MILs enter gendered spaces that are not accustomed to gender variance. Our vision is to have monthly discussion groups at the Ruth Ellis Center.

Consultation to agencies is something we wish to make available to the public. Once we lend our expertise and knowledge to the school that asked for our help, we will be on the road to assisting other schools, foster care centers, juvenile detention facilities, the prison system, and other institutions that may need our perspectives to help them carry out their goals to serve clients. This will enable us to provide cultural competency trainings for staff which will help protect the integrity of the LGBT youth/adults they serve.

Lastly, Activities/Outreach is our component that taps into our creativity and lightheartedness. It's a way to get as many MILs involved as possible to participate in some fun events for the community and to showcase their talents. The New Millennium Butches (New Jersey) sponsor an annual fashion show featuring Black MILs. This is an example of bristahs working together to build a sense of fellowship. The Jerry Palmer Group would like to do an annual fundraiser to benefit a worthy organization through activities. Our outreach to volunteers and allies will help to make this, and the other programs, happen.

Our priorities are self-care and self-insight. It starts with knowing self first which is why we established a series of "bootcamps" for anyone who wishes to become a volunteer. The bootcamp training curriculum gives us a chance to explore our multiple intersected identities on a deeper level and to celebrate our diversity as Black MIL's. We are very clear that being an MIL that is of African descent is an experience like no other in America and that being a woman requires us to seriously take a look at our ethical behavior towards one another as women, as lesbians, and as MILs. We believe in feminism/womanism and in doing so, we reject the negative hegemonic, patriarchal hetero attractional male forms of masculinity that is practiced by many men in their relations with women. We assert that a "female masculinity" is a legitimate, valid, and natural expression and that lesbians of color are able to tap into this expression in unique ways given our herstories and familiarity with the psychological experiences of being multiply intersected identities. Interrupting misogyny, sexism, and the objectification of women is something that we strive toward across all genders and attractionalities.

Furthermore, since we are a two-fold self-help and community service organization, we spend less time with justifying our existence to the public and more time placing our energies into being proactively involved in creating safe spaces for MILs in the Detroit area and making sure our voices/perspectives are not overlooked. Simultaneously, by virtue of who we are on the margins of society, we co-partner and collaborate with other groups in the struggle for equality. For example, we feel a kinship with our Black transmasculine and transgender brothers, and we affirm their journey, their walk, their transition, and we will continue to be their allies as they are to us. Together, we are breaking down barriers of the gender binary and all the "isms" that go along with those rigid barriers.

Ever since we started the Jerry Palmer Group in July of 2014, we have met with the school and formulated a plan of action to engage the students we were asked to work with. In order to properly prepare for any youth outreach endeavors, we created a boot camp training for MILs who wished to volunteer. The first one was conducted in August and the second one is scheduled for November. Before the end of July, our group facilitated a workshop at Hotter Than July—Detroit's Black LGBT Pride. In both August and September, we were guests on two different blog radio shows (Spiritually Speaking and Can We Talk for Real) and are currently invited to appear on a show in Atlanta. In October, we will be participating in a seminar on domestic violence in the lesbian community sponsored by Women Healing Women. We are grateful to those who have shown us support, taken us seriously, and expressed how worthy our mission is.

In just a short period of time, and only four monthly meetings so far, the group agreed upon the mission, the pledge, our motto, the five-point platform, and conducted bootcamp training, created our own handshake and cat call, and set up a Facebook Page! We are in the process of planning a dialogue between Black MILs and Black transmasculine and transgender men in Detroit. This whirlwind of continuous activity and monthly meetings could not be possible without the leadership cadre who are the women that stepped up to the plate and sacrificed their time, expertise, and energies. They are Elder Atiba Cohen, Brenda Hawkins, Rev. Inger Davis, Carolyn Simmons, Kunto Mawusi, and Markita Moore. Honorable mentions are Lisa Flagg, Jay Gold, Cynthia Thornton, and C'gar. These bristahs represent the best part of this whole process and that is the friendships and camaraderie that have evolved. We all look forward to getting together when it's just us fellas. (Note: We love our femme sistahs and we appreciate those femme allies that understand and value that we MILs have this time together for bonding.)

We realize that this first year is somewhat experimental in nature, and we will have to play it by ear with constant self-evaluation and plans to become a nonprofit at some point. Our hope is to become a template for others around the country who would like to start such a group and to be a voice where there is none. Needless to say, that we of the Jerry Palmer Group are honored to be the latest in joining the growing national movement of gender nonconforming women. We feel Jerry's spirit every time we chant our motto: "Women who dare to be themselves."

-Dr. Kofi Adoma

The Beginnings of bklyn boihood

In 2016, bklyn boihood has become a community of people that spans the globe. Together with each other or in collaboration with other dope queer people of color, we curate events, workshops, gatherings, trips, collaborations, meals, artistic opportunities for our community from NYC to Toronto, Boston, Detroit and beyond. At our best we are building media and frameworks of redefined masculinity to share, connecting intergenerationally and studying our history of queer, gender non-conforming Black and brown family everywhere. Today our online and in-person community has grown to tens of thousands of people. Our calendars have traveled to dozens of countries, our work has been featured from Bed Stuy to the Philippines. We have grown tremendously since 2009 both in our impact and size. *But we didn't start that way. We started out as just friends wondering why we were so weird and so unloved by the world.*

* * *

When Ryann Holmes and Genesis Tramaine established the collective, calling themselves "bois" was a decision that clapped back at the way people had hurled the word around like it was an insult. As if it meant we didn't fit or were unattractive or too physical or too chivalrous. Calling ourselves bois was a way of giving the finger to those who thought it hurtful, he used it with hate. But we are bois. bklyn boihood began as a space for masculinity to live in people who weren't cisgender males. (Cisgender = born "male" and identify as "male".) The collective grew in size and vision. Our mission expanded. The need to share the space and our work and our conversations grew.

We didn't fit in at gay nights at clubs. We didn't enjoy treating each other like men-with-machoism-to-prove. We collectively questioned why the idea that we could be beautiful, handsome, spiritual, soft and hard couldn't exist together. We liked making things together. We are artists, entrepreneurs, makers, dancers, performers, MCs, poets, graphic artists, students. Some of us were coming into our transmasculine identity. As we grew, bklyn boihood became a space where we could all exist and be affirmed and share ourselves as whole beings.

One thing we have not ever suffered from is the challenge of trying to look like or act like anyone else. The birth of this collective of studs, ags, tomboys, gender non conforming folk and transmen who believe that masculinity does not equal possession, violence, misogyny, machoism. For us it means checking our privilege, communicating, being openly loving of ourselves and each other, pushing back on bois who think disrespecting being a "boi" has to look one way for it to be authentic or who have bought into the notion that disrespecting women in words, thoughts and action makes them stronger or more believable.

Our existence outside of norms have always made our lives more complicated and infinitely more beautiful.

What if we put together a calendar to showcase the power and beauty and resilience of bois of color in our community? What would that do our conversations, stories, emotions and experiences? What if we created photo shoots that empower, opportunities to use their images for their own lives and uplift artists we know and love? What if we use what we have to throw parties for who we know? What if we could create small spaces where bois could feel free to dance, to feel vulnerable, to enjoy and to not replicate "straight club" experiences and others could feel safe in our presence? These questions are still the ones we apply to the work we're doing today. From these incredible calendars to parties to workshops and annual retreats—bklyn boihood's beginnings as a collective of bois who believed in our ability to more fully become ourselves, each other— and to, with confidence and love, demand that from the world.

But back in 2009 our politics were not fully formed. We were very young and still bumbling around the world, unconvinced that we really could be ourselves. As friends, through bklyn boihood we brought each other stories of awkward job interviews with ill-fitting clothes, really bad dates and complicated family exchanges. We all had the shared experiences of being both invisible to our families and hyper visible to police. There were daydreams of having lovers and families in ways that didn't fit in with conventions of not being "born male." There were our own histories of growing up queer, different, gay, as tombois and studs, doms, ag's. The beginnings of bklyn boihood are rooted in a time of realizing, first slowly and then more expansively, the presence and power of bois of color and the way we have existed all over the world, throughout all time. These things are still realities that have become cornerstones of who we are and how we move through the world.

There is magic in being able to have a collective of people traveling on similar journeys. There is power in giving those journeys the space to spread their wings into whatever it is we were each meant to become. Through our beginnings of conversations, of love, of fun, of supporting each other—our work birthed itself.

-Morgan Mann Willis

Untitled

Just when I thought I had found a comfortable space to exist, a perfect category to identify myself, an acceptable label that fits within the boundaries of my gender identity, and matched my gender expression, I am in the midst of yet another challenge. This challenge was brought on, and not so readily accepted, when I started shopping for a suit—the perfect suit to fit my body, my expression, my identity. I was looking for a suit that I could put on and feel damn good—one that makes me feel confident and still feel like I'm being true to my identity and my expression. I'm looking for an affordable suit that is not too tight and feminine, but not too loose that it will make me drown in the suit. Something in between; something that screams, I'm gender non-conforming, I'm queer, I'm trans*! Needless to say, I have yet to find that suit. I primarily wear 'men's clothing,' and sometimes I'll wear some 'women's' pieces, but I've also been looking at 'women's' and 'men's suits.' (I put these words and phrases in quotes, because I don't agree with placing people into boundaries and labeling their bodies based on the dimensions and fit of their clothing.)

Throughout my teenage and adult life, I've been searching for ways to label myself. This desire for a label spiraled out of control when people started misgendering me (when I cut my hair), and when people started asking me how I identify. If we lived in a society that didn't seek to separate people by inherent traits (genitalia, skin color, body type, ability, etc.), I mean, I'd be totally cool with existing in this space of 'human.' For the past few months, I've been existing as gender non-conforming, using feminine pronouns, trying out things that make me comfortable and not really thinking much about my gender identity. But then, I got a new job, and the dress code is business professional. So, I've been trying to find a way to still live in my true expression, and queer up the "business professional" workplace I'm entering.

Then, something even better happened. I found a solution to my problem, and it came in the form of support and compassion (and a little rolling of the eyes). I was venting to the person who has loved me unconditionally and who gives really awesome solicited and unsolicited advice all the time. In the midst of my breakdown about my gender identity crisis, my fiancé blurted out, "find a nice looking suit that you like, and get it tailored, dammit!

That's when I realized: the suit that I'm looking for doesn't exist. The label that I'm looking for doesn't exist. I must create a comfortable space for me and continue to tailor it, mend it and tend to it. Whether that suit is labeled for men or for women, I must find one that fits me and then get it fitted—queer it up. Because I'm queer; whether that queerness is labeled as gender non-conforming, unorthodox woman, boi, trans*, how I identify to myself and to the public is going to change as I grow and continue to knock down these gender insecurities. We all know that being lesbian, gay, bisexual, trans*, questioning, queer, pansexual, intersex, or even an ally—anything outside of society's comfortable box of 'normality'—will be a long lasting battle. In other words, it's hard to consistently love yourself while living outside the norm, especially when your existence is met with constant questioning and scrutiny. Nevertheless, it's a constant test that forces you to find comfort outside of your comfort zone. Through this new job and this suit struggle, I was reminded that, like life, gender is a journey, not an ultimatum. It's a journey that often seems like an unsolvable paradox. Most importantly, though, it's a journey that will challenge me to stay true to who I am and to how far I've come.

-Mi Register

Reflections on Race, Kinship, and Passing

A gaggle of white girls have been laughing for the entire 20 minutes that I've been waiting for the metro. I'm texting and have my headphones in, but I'm aware of their gaze.

"I dunno!" one squeals, looking at me.

Another responds, "I think it's a boy!"

They are laughing at me, I realize.

I squirm, and they laugh harder. They enjoy that I am uncomfortable.

I just cut my hair off a month ago, and this type of experience is new. I don't understand why a reasonable—is it?—confusion is so violent for me, or why it is such a source of entertainment for others. I feel detached from and ashamed of my body. I detach in order for the shame to not so fully belong to me. Never before have I felt disgusted by my own body, or dysphoric as I would later learn to call it.

Leaving the girls behind, I step onto the train upon its arrival and a white woman moves away from me hurriedly, as if afraid. I understand, by this action, that I have been read as male, but I don't understand how she arrived at this conclusion. I am small and have a soft face. I cannot harm her. I look too young to even be on the metro alone.

* * *

Everyone in the lobby of my dorm building is visibly drunk and trying to catch a body for the night. A guy runs towards me, laughing.

"Bruh! You wanna join our fraternity?"

I don't respond; I don't know how. I've come to believe that it is my responsibility to perform the gender I am read as. While navigating this potential threat, I also somehow experience a kind of sadistic pleasure. I know that when it is revealed that I am a woman, my life could be in danger. But I'm also amused by what triggers the realization, how it reveals the spectator's perception of gender. Such a realization repositions me as the spectator.

"It's called Broke Phi Broke!" He begins to step, something random he just made up, and I laugh—at what? His fraternity, the step, or him misgendering me?

He turns away from me and towards a girl sitting by the elevator who paid no attention to anything that just happened. His eyes widen, "Bruh! That's a girl! Oh shit!

But why the shock? Why the need to tell everyone else when only he (mis)gendered me? Why does the shock belong to him, but the knowledge of what violence that shock can produce only belong to me? This moment was not significant to him, maybe. Yet he never spoke to me again, even when I initiated conversation in passing or on the elevator. What influenced his assumption of my maleness, what disrupted it, and how did that disruption obliterate our initial kinship, which was both racialized and gendered? Rather than wholly alienating me from that kinship by informing others, why not react with, "My bad, sis"?

This moment connects me to the others that eject me from cis-normative racial kinship, and the hurt is amplified. My queerness, it is believed, is holding back black communities, emasculating black men. I am to blame for how my body reveals to the boy how fragile and useless the standards of his masculinity are.

* * *

These two experiences were not the most violent or transformative, but they demonstrate the conglomerate of things that come together to produce a (mis)reading of my gender. It's been two years since both of these events have happened, and as I become more comfortable in gender performance, I think of these and ongoing situations more thoroughly, and even metacognitively.

When I pass as male, I know that I am simply passing, not being. But the spectator doesn't. So while I am experiencing the privilege of being read and treated as male, I am also moving through public spaces being read as black male. Because I am socialized to know how to respond to violence against black female bodies, when I pass I am entering a world that I do not know how to defend myself from. The phallus that I am assumed to have, which is of course a cis-sexist reading of my body, and able to use as a weapon, is not present. This begs the question of what is male, and my contextual choice to refer to this as passing versus being misgendered.

Oliver Bendorf's exploration of "passing," as follows, has been useful to me as I unpack my experiences:

> *What interests me most is that this same word — "pass" — signifies identity trouble and a moving through or around; it's no wonder we use it as a euphemism for dying. Pass, to go by, to cross over, to step (from pace), to go on, move forward, make one's way. To experience, undergo. To be thought to be something one is not. To decline, refuse. To not fail.*

What interests me most of Bendorf's thoughts is the idea of not failing. When I first started being read as male, I understood it as being misgendered—having failed. I was used to my public performance of womanhood being "good enough," and felt dangerously visible by this sudden change in how my gender was read. I had considered transitioning before and knew that I identified as masculine of center, and now I felt like everyone knew that and was pressuring me to transition or change my presentation sooner. In this way, passing also came as a strange gift that gave me the space to actualize the ways in which I never agreed to being or performing as a woman. While many black girls and women speak to the structural denial of their womanhood and femininity, my experience has been that femininity has been forced upon me, particularly as I've moved away from it. Primarily, those forcing femininity on me were the women and girls who felt their own had been denied to them. Aunties and other female relatives often inquire incredulously about my hair; pressure me to wear dresses and other "feminine" clothing, and sometimes flat out tell me to be more ladylike. I understand that their forcefulness is due to their own trauma, though still no less offensive and at times traumatizing for me. Just as spectators initially violently gendered me as male, in an attempt to "put me in my place," female relatives often pressure me to perform in feminine ways. Both actions I believe work to emphasize how much of a communal performance gender is. The spectator is affirmed in his or her gender performance if mine aligns with or compliments it and does not push the boundaries of what can be. In this way, I've come to understand gender as deeply racialized and about forging a particular kind of public and private kinship based on who achieves gender by varying standards.

Sources

Bendorf, Oliver. "After I Came Out As A Transgender Man, I Was Asked If It Felt Like I Had Died." BuzzFeed. 20 Jan. 2014. Web. 30 Sept. 2014. <http://www.buzzfeed.com/oliverbendorf/after-i-came-out-as-a-transgender-man>

-L.G. Parker

Beautiful, beautiful scars.

I remember feeling scared when I was young that my parts weren't put together right. That somehow somewhere along the way the pieces got dropped on the floor and put together all wrong out of haste. Maybe my brain wasn't the right one or my body was wrong but either way I just knew that my pieces were put together different than everyone else. I remember hearing people ask why I wore "boys clothes" and wanted "boys toys" and I thought the obvious answer was that I must be obviously be a boy. But people would laugh. "You're not a boy, don't be dumb."

And so I learned that I wasn't. I started working on accepting that obviously I wasn't a boy because my parts didn't add up right. I had the right brain, the right heart but my body was fleshy in all the wrong places and went out where it should have gone in and went in where it should have gone out. I got used to hating my body. I got used to buying clothes that tricked my eyes into seeing what my heart and my brain and my soul saw in myself and pretended that it was all okay. I let people throw labels at me like "dyke" and "butch" even though I never really felt them stick. They'd slide off my flesh that was all wrong and disappear. I got used to people looking hard at me when I walked by them and hearing little voices from little mouths ask their moms and dads, "is that a boy or a girl?" I got used to asking myself that question a lot too.

I fought for 18 long years to get used to being uncomfortable with my body that was fleshy in all the wrong places and went out where it should go in and go in where it should go out. Then one day I saw him for the first time. I don't know his name or his story but he was beautiful. He had stubble on his chin that was round like mine, and he had scars on his chest where his body that was fleshy in all the wrong places used to be.

Beautiful, beautiful scars.

He was holding a syringe in his hands and was injecting something into his legs that were hairy like mine and smiling to himself like he was happy. I cried for an hour straight. I looked for more pictures of boys and bois whose names and stories I'd never know and I felt something I had never felt before. I felt hope.

I told my friends, my parents, my baby sister and myself the thing that I'd always known but this time they believed me. I'm a boy, I told them. Yes, you are they reassured me. And then I started telling everyone I met and for the first time in my entire life I felt happy in a way that I never thought I would feel. I bought a shirt that made my body that was fleshy in all the wrong places go in where it had gone out. I saw a counselor. Then another. I bought a piece of silicone that made my parts that went in where they should have gone out look like they went out.

Then I saw an endocrinologist. Then the counselor again. I got syringes and started injecting something into my legs that are now hairy forests. Then I saw a surgeon. I fought my insurance. I won. I picked a date. Seven days before Christmas. I told my friends and they promised to help me afford it. They started a crowdfunding page and raised over $700 in 24 hours. I cried more. The tears dripped down my round face with stubble like the boy in the picture I had seen and I smiled the way he had smiled. I touched my chest where I knew I would have scars like him. Beautiful, beautiful scars.

-Marcus Bethel

Sex

On longing the fantastical

My secret dreams *Craigslist* ad goes:

*"brown amerikan mixed-race tender queer tibo
(former teenage beauty queen at heart) transman
seeks kindred yet platonic times w/ someone similar.
If you have stances on palabok recipes or the emo
nature yet sexism of pinoy rock music, appreciate
the patterns of bow ties and banigs, please give me
a shout. priority will be given to those who don't
want any political bullshit, who are for justice
without the righteousness. would love someone
who has a thing or two to say about contemporary
pinoy cuisine via diasporic interpretation or mixed
race   manhood.   rigid   gender   assumptions   and
amerikan
vegetarians who won't dabble in lechon once in a blue
moon, will not be contacted."*

-Kay Ulanday Barrett

Stud Slayer

I'm known for a lot of things but what I'm known mostly for is the advocacy, acceptance and visibility of stud for stud (masculine women who date other masculine women). Although that is a huge part of who/what I am, what I care most about is the acknowledgement, affirmation and empowerment of the sexuality of masculine identified women of color because this isn't just an s4s issue, but a masculine women of all preferences issue. In laymen's terms, I want studs/doms/ AGs/butches/bois to not only be comfortable in their own sexuality and sexual expression but to affirm and support their fellow bois in their journey to owning and loving their sexuality. I advocate this in the form of queer porn by only performing with masculine women of color and also bottoming (allowing another boi to penetrate/fuck me).

Masculinity is such a fragile construct for black lesbians who identify on that spectrum. All too often the examples of masculinity we are subjected to daily are all the negative ones. Masculine women of color often practice and promote patriarchy, misogyny, slut/body shaming, abuse of all kinds, all in the name of 'masculinity' and being 'bois.' Why? Because that's what we're conditioned to believe is the appropriate way of masculine expression. These negative behaviors have seeped into the bedroom to the point bois believe showing any signs of submissiveness (being penetrated in any way, moaning 'like a girl,' or lying in a position of submission) is akin to being weak and a 'bitch' therefore not being a 'real' boi. My passion is showing and telling bois that their sexual wants/needs/desires do not diminish their boihood but enhances it. Being masculine and showing their natural feminine traits that they try so hard to oppress/suppress for whatever reason can live in a symbiotic relationship. Bois will find that if they embrace them both they will have a better quality of life and sex life.

Recently I had an experience that confirmed, validated and affirmed my advocacy as not only legit but *much* needed. I've never shared my personal experiences believing my porn performances and personal blog would be enough to make my point. But here is a unique opportunity to really 'practice what I preach.' Here's my story:

I'm 36 years old now (I don't normally tell my age but it's relevant to this story). Around the age of 33, I started going through a lot of changes. I noticed I wanted to be less masculine or at least not be 'on' all the time. I wasn't so pressed to act in a hyper-masculine manner even when others around me were doing so. I didn't need to be the 'alpha' all the time, for that role can be draining. I noticed I dealt with men differently and they dealt with me differently as well. Instead of coming across as aggressive and therefore 'challenging' their masculinity, I would say I would subtly submit, or be flirtatious. *Whoa!* I got more flies with that honey! I was actually amused by it. For the first time in forever, maybe even ever, I was using my femininity to get the things I wanted. Guess what? I liked it! And I didn't feel less of a boi for doing it.

With that I noticed my sexual needs were evolving and changing. I wanted to top less and bottom more. Now I am known as a hardcore top. *I can lay some pipe.* Everyone knows this. But I was known as a hardcore top not because that's what I preferred, but because I had never found the one I trusted enough to 'handle' me. She had to have the 'look' and the skillset before I would open my legs and submit willingly and totally.

Well I found her... rather she found me. Whatever energy I was putting out in the universe she picked up on and reached out to me. She knew who I was but, despite that, she was able to see past the 'persona' and pick up on exactly what I needed. I really appreciated that she didn't care about porn or 'Stud Slayer' or even my dick! She wanted to know who I was, who Kai was. That was the foundation for the trust that was to build the platform that she could raise me on, to fulfill my sexual desires. I absolutely love masculine women. The more masculine looking, the better and she was definitely what I liked. She was taller, stronger, and bigger than me which was something I've never experienced with another woman. She was a true alpha, in stance, build and confidence. Quite frankly she made my pussy wet. She exuded confidence and although she never bragged or discussed her bedroom resume, my instinct told me she was the truth...she could fuck.

Her muscles, her stature, her stance were just beautiful. She was beautiful in a very masculine, dominating way. I wanted to submit to her. I wanted to give myself to her. I trusted her. I wanted her. I needed her. As she entered me and I gasped, I felt a release! I felt light...free. I wasn't confined to the persona that was Stud Slayer or the role of being a top. I could let go and be taken care of which is something I wasn't used to. I was allowed to express myself in a way I had never been comfortable doing. I didn't feel less of a boi for it either. I felt empowered actually. She affirmed me in so many ways. She showed it was okay to be me, even though that's what I preach and advocate about all day, it's different when you can actually feel and do it. I felt my femininity coming out but in a masculine way, if that makes any sense.

At first glance one would think we were two gay men fucking, but we were bois... beautiful, black, bois caught in a moment of affirmation, validation and ecstasy. We were affirming our individual needs, validating our masculinity from another peer, another alpha, and in the throes of pure pleasure and ecstasy. At the risk of not sounding too cocky, at that moment I knew what it was like for the bois who had been with me before. The look on their faces and the astonishment in their eyes of having been fucked in a way that they could never believe could happen in real life, but could only dream about, was the exact look I'm sure I had. I was now experiencing that euphoria. I felt complete. My womanhood was colliding with my boihood and believe it or not, they not only got along but worked together and thrived as a team.

I've always felt that void, that I was missing

something, that desire I had yet to fulfill, the need to relax and be me, whichever way that manifested. I knew it was what other bois wanted and craved as well. I knew I couldn't be the only one, hence why I started becoming more vocal about it. I'm not sharing this story because I like spilling my feelings in the air. I'm sharing this story because I want other bois to look at me and find the courage and strength to step out there and demand their sexual needs be met and seek out people who can give them what they want (no matter how they identify or present). *I am a boi. I am a stud. I am masculine presenting. I am an Alpha.* Yet despite all these things (or because of them), *I am still a woman. I redefine and reaffirm masculinity every day. This is my truth.*

-Kai Brown (aka Stud Slayer)

A Body Worthy of Desire

Since the day I was born my body has defined my experience, commitment, and activism. At the age of 25, I received my medical records from Columbia-Presbyterian Medical Center. After months of waiting, unreturned phone calls, and lost medical record request forms I finally got a manila envelope in the mail, opened it and began scanning the dense packet of information. I read doctor's notes, surgeon's notes, and other information related to my birth. The records included the length of my phallus along with descriptions of my scrotum and palpable, but undescended, testicles. The doctors also noted that I had "ambiguous" genitalia, which was later crossed out and replaced with "normal." Based on the size of my genitals and the medical community's commitment to the gender binary, I was assigned female.

In the records was written: "In the interest of proper psychosexual orientation of the infant, and in order to protect the parent's emotional well being, the mother has been told that: 1. The baby is a girl and will function as such.

2. She has gonads which require removal in the future (not testes)."

My mother would later tell me that when she brought me home from the hospital the Pediatric Endocrinology Clinic at Columbia-Presbyterian harassed her for a couple of weeks about bringing me in for surgery to remove my undescended testes. She wondered, "Why are these people harassing me so much?" My mother's resistance alone spared me from surgery until I was much older.

I was a rambunctious and curious kid. I ran around the house shirtless, beating my chest with declarations that I was a boy. I thought I was a boy until I was seven and my mom, through words and dresses, reinforced my assignment as female. I hated dresses with a passion and would always reach for my corduroy overalls in place of a dress any day.

I always marveled at the size of what doctors referred to, as an "enlarged clitoris," and I knew the bodies of my female playmates were different from mine. Whenever they saw my "clitoris" they remarked at its appearance and were amazed that I could pee standing up. This "bathroom ability" distinguished me from other girls and, despite my mother's efforts, confirmed for me that I was indeed a boy.

When I was eight years old my mom talked to me about having "Testicular Feminization Syndrome." Of course, at that age I didn't know what that was or what that meant for my body. I didn't know how different I was until my period failed to arrive. One morning at the age of 11, I had spots of blood in my underwear and I thought that my period had finally come. I was living with my sister in North Carolina at the time and she told me that young women get their period around my age. I was scared. I didn't know what to do. She bought me Maxi pads and advised me to wear them during my period. I only used one. The trickle of blood stopped and since I didn't have any more signs of menstruation, there was nothing more to talk about. I don't have a medical explanation for it, but from what I understand it's just something that weirdly happens.

My intersex trait would resurface again when a painful urinary tract infection landed me in a doctor's office. The doctor told my sister that she "did not observe a vagina." My sister told the doctor about the trait in my family now known as Androgen Insensitivity Syndrome (AIS).

I am one of seven people in my family living with this trait. AIS is an intersex trait where the infant is born with XY chromosomes and undescended testicles, but the external genitalia appear female, ambiguous, or as an underdeveloped male. There are variations in the severity of AIS that range from Complete Androgen Insensitivity Syndrome (CAIS) to Mild Androgen Insensitivity Syndrome (MAIS). I fell somewhere in the middle having been exposed to androgens in the womb. However, in the eyes of my doctors, I did not masculinize "enough" to be assigned male.

So much of me was shrouded in secrecy. Because of pain related to my undescended testicles, they were removed when I was 13. Barely out of surgery, and in excruciating pain, a team of residents came into my room to look at the fresh wounds and, also, to examine my genitals. I was not only subject to an invasive medical procedure, but was doubly violated by the prying eyes of mostly male residents examining my half-naked pubescent body. These examinations, borne of curiosity and fascination, continued for me as an adult when physicians would often want to get a look at my genitals even when my visit was for something totally unrelated like a cold.

I didn't find out the specifics of my birth until sophomore year of college when I searched "Testicular Feminization Syndrome" online. The information that came up on the screen referred to Testicular Feminization Syndrome as Androgen Insensitivity Syndrome. Reading the descriptions of the physical characteristics of people with AIS I was both shocked and relieved: a combination leaving me profoundly sad and afraid.

That was perhaps my worst semester in college. I felt paralyzed with this new information and I avoided sex and dating altogether. Despite being one of the "big dykes on campus," I avoided any sexual contact that involved nudity. Whenever I did have sex with women, I touched them. I did not allow them to touch me. That worked for the most part until I was a senior and started dating a woman who was as interested in making love to me as I was to her. Just the thought of that terrified me. Before we had sex for the first time I tearfully called home only to meet with my mother's own limitations in explaining how I could negotiate sex with an intersex body. She had no answers for me.

When my new girlfriend and I eventually had sex, we discovered neither of us really knew what we were doing. With the very real disconnection I felt from my own body, and my overall sexual inexperience, I was a horrible lover. After that relationship ended I continued to have sexual relationships devoid of connection and sexual pleasure. My relationship with my body and sexuality was colored by the unmonitored prejudices of doctors, growing up Black, poor and queer which all contributed to a deep sense of being unlovable.

I chose women who were curious about my body but daunted at the prospect of trying to please me. I didn't have a vagina, a G-spot, a penis, or a prostate. I felt incapable of sexual pleasure. I didn't experience my first orgasm until the age of 25. Prior to taking testosterone I would fantasize about women and sex, but didn't have any sexual urges since I didn't have any sex hormones in my body. My first orgasm was with a woman who was patient with me, and advocated for my pleasure. She listened to my body's rhythm with every move that she made. Before her I did not feel desired or worthy of the time it might take not only for me to orgasm but for my different body to be explored with respect.

I moved to the Bay Area when I was 24, legally changed my name, started taking
testosterone, and reaffirmed my gender as male. The transition to manhood was a leap of faith. I decided to transition because I felt my body already moving in that direction prior to my testicles being removed at 13. My transition was an act against the path prescribed for me by the medical community. For the most part, infants with Androgen Insensitivity Syndrome are assigned female but in reality at least 20% of those assigned female will transition to live as male.

The physical part of my transition was not easy. As my transgender brothers were celebrating the gender-affirming effects of testosterone I was experiencing estrogenic effects of excess testosterone such as tender breasts, water retention, and weight gain. My body was reacting that way because of my partial sensitivity to testosterone. I soon realized that my transition as an intersex person was different. It was then that I started to identify more with being an intersex person distinguishing myself from the transgender community. For the longest time, the FTM community provided a space for me to connect with other men who were raised and socialized as female, but I realized that I needed to step out and claim my place as an intersex man in this world.

When I discovered masturbation, I started to connect with my intersex body and became more determined than ever to reclaim it. The unfamiliar became known, and the estranged part of me came home. I felt more confident. I was emboldened by my newfound sexual freedom. I learned how to touch myself and masturbated all of the time. I felt like a young person experiencing puberty. Over time my focus on masturbation became obsession and I unknowingly started to feed a growing addiction I had to sex.

It started with responding to sexual ads posted on *Craigslist*. Then I started watching porn. The obsession with sex was not confined to the privacy of my mind or my bedroom, but spilled out into my office and work life. Like the addict that I was, the signs were painfully obvious that my life was spinning out of control. The justification for all of this was that I had been denied this pleasure for so long and eventually I would tire out and move on. Over time, though, it became clear that no matter how much sex I had it was never enough.

By the time I sought professional help, I couldn't think straight. I was walking around in a haze of confusion and sadness. I felt alone. I was having an affair with a co-worker, flirting with a married woman, and having sex with people I met online. I eventually "bottomed out" and talked to a woman at my job that was also a therapist. She recommended several therapists. By sheer chance I randomly chose one who had over 15 years in sexual recovery. After hearing me talk about my sordid sexual life, he pointed me toward a 12-step program for sexual addiction. At first, I refused to believe I was an addict of any kind. After only a handful of meetings I began to see that my life had become unmanageable as a result of my sexual pursuits. I eventually shed many of those behaviors with the help of a sponsor, meetings, and working the steps, leaving me with the challenge of building a healthy sexuality that did not rely on external validation.

I know my sexual addiction is not a result of being born with AIS. I suspect, though, it might be a byproduct of the prejudicial medical treatment I received and unaddressed trauma. My addiction to sex is a function of the violence that I witnessed both at home and in my community. This manifested as cycles of substance use, incarceration and dysfunctional interpersonal relationships. However, one of the more resounding messages that I received from society and medical providers was that my Black, queer, working class, intersex body was not enough. From an early age I was told that my body was different. Doctors instructed my mother that my intersex status was not to be discussed with anyone except other doctors.

Many times in a doctor's office I would lie there as they examined my genitals in ways that were unapologetic and disrespectful. Unfortunately, these are not isolated experiences. So many of my friends with intersex traits have been subjected to the same treatment or have endured much worse. I say to myself and other intersex people reading this: We are worthy of deep desire and profound respect. The journey home has not been easy. Although our bodies may have been altered from their unique and faultless beginnings, we are worthy of being held, pleasured, and explored with respect and boundaries. In short, fulfilled.

In a radical awakening of our sexual desires and prowess we have the right to choose celibacy or not, kink or vanilla, top/bottom or switch, monogamy or polyamory, queerness or non-queerness. I demand our right to be fully incorporated and embodied human beings.

-Sean Saifa M. Wall

Beautiful Tall Boy

"Tongues, suck, kiss, lick, bite, cock, nipples, squeeze, fuck, tight, wet, fingers,
bind, slippery, ass, moan, grab... what are you into?
Me: Black FTM (meaning female-to-male trans man), muscular, facial hair, nice
body... and horny as hell.
You: Horny guy, sexually adventurous, know what FTM means and loud as fuck
when you come.
Respond with a face picture or you don't get a response from me."

It was a cold cloudy fall day in 2010 when he responded to my *Craigslist* ad and decided to visit me in my Brooklyn apartment. Beautiful, tall black boy. Six feet something. Long bushy hair, tamed into a ponytail at the back of his head. Chestnut colored skin. Pale brown almond shaped eyes. I snagged him during my desperate search for the one or a someone to satisfy the itch I'd get more often than I care to admit. An itch that would crawl inside me, into the smallest space of me and lodge. In response I'd do all I could to scratch, frequently trolling hook-up sites for hours, staring at partially nude pictures of black cis men on adam4adam, manhunt, and others, browsing through profiles written by equally desperate horny types trying their damnedest to come off apathetic. Or I'd hit *Craigslist* and answer all the "looking for a Trans Man" ads I could find where the author didn't sound like a serial killer. Many times they did. So I'd pen my own ad, making it extra pervy because I wanted the deep lust coursing through me to come off loud and clear. The authors of *Craigslist* personals are serious dabblers in the explicit, the vulgar, and the profane, so I strived to ink something worthy of that ilk, an ad that effectively conveyed my raunchy yearnings to be fucked and be demeaned in all the sexual ways that I like. The responses, over time ceased to surprise me. They were from married heterosexual men with a thing for trans guys of color or bisexual men on the DL or men who couldn't get it up and would much rather bury their head in my boi pussy and lose track of time or dominant hung tops who are neither bi, gay, nor straight or men who, in the words of one responder, are "99% gay but like pussy every once a while."

"Hey mama, hit me back. I can fuck you good."

That email and its various iterations were immediately deleted. I could put up with a lot when I'm in a desperate horny state, but what I would not condone was being mis-gendered.

"I'm so hard right now because of your ad."

These I kept, especially if there was something complicated about the emailer. Was he married? Was he on the DL? Was he much older? Did he have an indefinable sexuality? Something not wrapped up in a pretty bow of "gay" or "bisexual" or hell, even "queer" (in the ubiquitous ways it's used these days)? Did he offer something that could properly afford the description illicit? Sleeping with sexually confused men was inexplicably alluring, even though half the time the confused part got in the way of the fucking part.

By the time the beautiful tall black boy came over, I'd already honed my craft of submerging reason and denouncing truth. The raised eyebrows and startled expression on his face when I opened the door told me everything right away. That and the "you're more masculine than I thought." He doesn't want to be associated with what we are about to do. "Do you go down?" I asked him after he'd followed me from my doorway though the hallway, through the railroad-style bedrooms, into mine.

"I gotta know you better to do something like that," he responded after planting his ass on my full size bed, and I sat beside him taking in his eyes. I was looking for head and I'd made that quite clear in my ad. In our back and forth, he'd listed that as one of his go-to's as we picked a day, time and location. Yet here he was, haughty expression and all, backing out. I tried not to think about what that meant. I tried not to face this version of me that would sleep with someone whose aversion for me couldn't be distinguished from his attraction. The weed I'd smoked earlier had dulled that rational part of my brain and heightened the part that does the feeling. Once again, my well-practiced craft, thought suppression, was hard at work.

"Take off your clothes."

His sneer distorted his features, translating loud

and clear. "I don't want to be here." He didn't want to do me but he was going to let his libido get the best of him. His disgust should have given me pause, and it did. It should have forced the words ,"Get the fuck up outta' my house" from my mouth, but it didn't. Instead I stripped and obeyed him when he gestured for me to turn around and pushed me onto the bed. I clambered on and got on fours, butt up in the air, primed for entry. I felt him slip in. I won't lie, it felt good.

There's something about the mix of shame and lust that eggs me on, gets me wetter and harder in spite of myself. I can trace its roots to that moment, back home in Port Harcourt. My parents were out for the afternoon, while Tunde and I were nowhere to be found. After I was all grown up, better able to stomach the reality of this part of my childhood, my elder sister told me how she searched the house for us, looking on the top floor where my bedroom took up one of the four corners of the house. She walked through the ground floor calling out our names. We weren't in the living room or the kitchen, Tunde's favorite room in the house. She stuck her face out the kitchen window and called out but we weren't in the expansive backyard either. Then she decided to try his room, also on the ground floor, but there's no reason we'd be in there...

"What are you doing?!"

My sister's open mouth formed an 'O,' a perfect circle, her skinny frame standing in the doorway like a beanpole planted in the mud. One hand clasped the doorknob, holding the door wide open, while the other dangled aimlessly by her side.

Tunde and I were on the floor of his bedroom.

More words poured out of her mouth, but I couldn't hear them, surrounded as I was by a thick wall of shame. The door slammed shut behind her and opened again almost immediately as he ran after her. I was left alone in his sienna-painted room, on my knees, my pants bunched down my thighs, butt exposed.

I was seven.

I slipped on my clothes and followed them into the dining room where my sister folded her frame into one of the lime green cushioned chairs surrounding the long oval glass dining table. The room was awash in bright yellow light courtesy of the sun blazing through windows that spanned an entire wall.

"Please don't tell them."

Now it was him on his knees, begging her in a high-pitched voice I'd never heard him use before, his breaths coming out in loud spurts. My sister shook her head over and over like she was trying to shake this new memory of us out of her head.

She never told.

He stopped forcing me to visit him eventually. After he'd left Port Harcourt for the US, escaping the ugly memory of us, I spent my pre-teen and early teen years acting out our perverted games, rubbing up against the older men who worked for us, trying to continue some legacy I thought was mine because of what he'd initiated between us.

A few years later after my sister walked in on us, my dad's promotion at work brought with it a fancy big house in Port Harcourt. It was painted pure white inside and out, surrounded by a huge perfectly manicured green lawn that forced a gasp out of me. This was the biggest house we'd lived in yet. After getting transferred from city to city, from prestigious oil company job to even more prestigious oil company job, this big white house with its accompanying large lawn, showed just how far up my dad had climbed.

I was trying to turn over a new leaf. 12 years old, new town, new house, and new class of men working for us. It was time for a change, but how do you change a way of being that had ruled your life since age seven? I wanted to stop whoring, but long ago a light switch had been flipped on and turning it off was something I didn't have the tools to do yet. It didn't stop in Warri, where we'd lived before moving to the big house in Port Harcourt. Where me and Patience, our 15-year housegirl at the time, flirted with and nearly fucked old man Ezekiel, with his yellowed gunk-lodged teeth and his smile that evoked in me equal parts lust and disgust. Or the old gardener who did things to me in the shed where we kept the wheelbarrow, shovels and gardening tools. Or the houseboy we had briefly, who was probably only a few years older than me. One day he spit in my mouth all under the guise of kissing me, but we won't talk about that.

Those acts of sex, confusing in their mix of nonconsensual and consensual, seemed to lead me to the encounter with the beautiful tall black boy. Shame, my ever present and dutiful companion, sat in the corner of the bed looking at us as we fucked like zoo-ed creatures responding to a primal urge with no care for the bars surrounding us. He fucked me like he didn't give a fuck if I liked it or not, which unwittingly meant that I liked it even more. The reckless-abandon and do-what-you will-ness we drew around us like a safety blanket and hung on hard. At one point I looked back at him and this time his face was distorted, not by disgust, but deep pleasure. Teeth bared and clenched, his eyes opening and closing. Opening and closing as if to the rhythm of his penetrations. I enjoyed that too. Shame aside, there's something about a person's look of pure ecstasy that gets me going, almost as much as fucking itself. I think I came that day but I don't remember. He certainly did. We didn't say anything to each other as he left. And in that silence, shame—my steady companion, climbed down from the bed and followed us to the door.

In the years since, I've been working with this shame that's as old as my memories of abuse. It's an all-pervasive thing, there when I interact with friends, co-workers, family and random people on the street, lurking, infusing my interactions with heightened self-consciousness and stilting my expressions. Its hands are entangled in my vocal chords, strangling my words. When I sit on the cushion to meditate, childhood memories of muddied sexual encounters hit me like Molotov cocktails, over and over, showing me shame's myriad flavors.

There's the shame that masquerades as shyness, the shame that's merged with anger and rage, the shame that dissolves into self-deprecating humor. All of these foes appear to me, and one by one, repeatedly, I work with turning them into friends. The seven-year-old and teenage me that suffered through abuse and perpetual re-traumatization and the adult trans masculine me that's been stooped over by the burden of silence all these years, they both take center stage in these moments and I see how ashamed I was, is. How

159

alone I felt, in the midst of deep pain and confusion about the things being done to my body. How ignored and mishandled I was by the people supposedly charged with my care.

I'm learning to give that child the safety and love she lacked. I'm learning to forgive this trans masculine adult when the past revisits the present.

-Ola Osaze

Dying To Be Me

Better to die fighting for freedom
Than be a prisoner all the days of your life
-- Bob Marley

When I was young we'd play house
My earliest memory of this
Was between 4 and 6
And every time I was the daddy
And Nafeesah was my chick
And every time she, her sister and brother
Would spend the night
Muhammad would catch us
Under the blanket in a deep, passionate
Five-year-old version of a kiss
Well she was seven
I suppose I've always had a thing for older women
I digress…

We'd imitate what
leading actors and actresses on the Soap Operas would do
so Young and Restless
And she was Bold N Beautiful
And when I was
I gave her a sweet tart necklace

161

Because being her boyfriend
Was a matter of exhibiting and establishing commitment
And even at such a young age
I harnessed male patriarchy and privilege

My idol
At the time was Bobby Brown
So I'd call her my tender roni
Until our tender moment were interrupted
When her mother found us in the play house naked
And it's so difficult to explain
What you feel so strongly Mother Nature chose to create

I was four years old

The first time I attempted to stand up and urinate
Imagine clutching your pubic region
In your tiny hands hoping it will transform into a penis

Because Jeris and Dorian have one
And the three of you look like boys
Act like boys
Wish I could dress like the boys
Picture
Stuffing your flower patterned panties with socks
Because this
Is what the grown men who modeled briefs in the JC
Penney's catalog have
And lowering your voice
And tucking your flowy mane of hair under your
grandfather caps
Because the rat race of living as a girl has led you to a
mouse trap

And chasing the proverbial cheese
Of something you'll never be
But feel
Leaves you feeling ill

The face of a young boy with the tone of one as well

Despising puberty
A process young girls usually
Welcome
I watched breasts swell
Over summers

Wishing they came with receipts
To make myself whole
I desired to cut off half of me
On bended knee
I'd request the same prayer
To wake up reconstructed
No longer binding away my blues
No longer pacing breaths
Because inhaling and exhaling is all about technique

And the wrappings so tight my lungs and chest feel
infused
Decreasing circulation throughout bodily tissues
Indentations stretching from beneath to armpits
Into rib cages that are bruised
No longer duct taping C cups
But bearing a well-contoured chest with an opportunity
to say

My nuts
Can't breathe
Because my underwear are too tight
But instead I spend my days on some sort of life support
Passing
An FTM

Passing
Transman
Passing
Transguy
T Man
The irony of transitioning
Also associated with death

And each day that I pass
A major part of me dies
While in strangers eyes I appear cis
(For those unaware
Cis means biologically)

And though I blend with most boys and a few men
My mind and spirit are in conflict with my anatomy
So financially I invest in me
Little by little
Bench pressing until my menstruating
Eventually stops
The price of a double front chest compression shirt
$24.95 plus shipping and handling
Handles my breasts until handling is something I can opt
Out of

An STP so I can stand to pee
$54.99 even available in the same complexion as me
And after all of these adjustments and prosthetics
Squeezing the life out of me

I've lightened my perspective
And to top it all off
With a cocktail of testosterone
I'm injected

Everyday of my life
To maintain the type of life
I've always wanted to have

The cutting of flesh
Fresh removal of breasts
And at some point
A hysterectomy

Because doctors suggest this will be best
Since in essence the longer my body ingest
This vitamin of T
My reproductive system basically dries up
Which can be detrimental to me

Imagine being 28 beginning puberty
Emotional instability
Where the slightest dosage inaccuracy
Can cause tragedy

So I lift
I pack and bind
And pack
And endure growing pains

As I watch my mother's daughter fade
And the only resembling factor is a hint of
Sparkle left in my eyes
Because every time I go under
Providing my own anesthesia yet slicing my own wrist
Where blades inflict and slit
Where there's the necessity
Of surgery
Formally changing all legal documents
Creating a nightmarish fallacy of memories for my parents
Because according to these papers
I've been this way ever since
Birth
Passing
Similar to post slavery
And brown paper bag test
Shackles removed

Dying to be free with every ounce of blood transfused
The abrasions and contusions
Trauma and prescriptions
But there's a big difference between living and surviving
And I'm dying to experience existence

I've been told
Your body is your temple
So this poem is for folks like me
Who alter our altars
To discover its fine finishings
Trimming away and chiseling
Doing this in remembrance
Of the little boy dwelling within
Who inscribes
DNR on his past

Because everyday he takes steps
Towards the tip of the ledge
Of this hypothetical roof
Where jumping is the only option
And the echoing of my swallowing
Resounds loud as rolling seas
See
This is where
Freshly scrubbed
Then towel dried
Once wet feet
Meet
Bathroom carpeting
Carefully placed over tile
To avoid slip ups
never revealing the caulk
sealing it
holding it
joining each piece together
where
the concealing
where building and foundation greet
can't be seen
without the seams
being pulled apart
the heart of this structure
losing the rhythm
the tightly clenched fist
folding the tiniest of putty into cement
imagine what was frozen in time
microorganisms tucked into the grains of concrete
what I wouldn't give to feel
complete

online funding sources set up for alterations amounting
to tuition
I'm still learning life's courses
erasing water from limbs
staring at this flower
wondering if I'm smothering its blossoming
but if my petals are drooping and toppling
what good is your offered sunlight
and hydration
if my soil and seeds
don't compliment and accompany
my opening at daybreak

and I hope you don't notice
when you see me
I'm all cramped up
so many bandages
and bruises
I panic and patch me up
so much unloaded baggage
at some point I packed me up
see it's at this moment
when I stand before the mirror
slightly blanketed in just enough steam
where attempts to wipe it away
make it worse
and the discourse
of evaluating anything above or below
my torso
is impossible
besides
by the time
the film fades

I've compressed
my breasts
kidneys
liver
stomach
intestines
bladder
heart
lungs
spine
into the confines
of elasticity
because
passing
is just as much apart of living
as it is dying
the irony
but in transitioning
I am free
essentially
dying to be
me

-Royce Hall

Untitled

We are soldiers of a mutual struggle
Fighting the same standstill battle
We relate
She is she and I am not there yet
She shows me her true hate
Hers and mine are alike
She takes her frustration out on me
but all I want is for her to take away the confusion
So she strips me of my binding security
And reminds me of what I am
 It's like looking in a mirror
 I submit
She debriefs me
and acknowledges my curves
She tells me I'm beautiful as she straps up
In this moment we are authentic

I grab the top of her yellow fade and bring her closer
Our tongues break dance
What time is it?
It is show time
She takes hold of my thick deception
and feels for my limit
 I have none

So she gives It to me hard
and then harder
    I give it right back
She makes me feel welcome
In this moment we identify

Our rhythm echoes
As she encourages my penetrating moans
and embraces my soft cues
She fucks me until I'm raw
Until I can take no more
Until I release
Until the sheets are stained with our defiance
Until we are two tired bois
She loves this shit
    and I love her because she validates my existence
Because she is everything that I am
But I am not there yet

-Noel Will

Ruminate

There's this little alarm that goes off in my head every second Thursday. It'll probably be going off every second Thursday until I die. I used to like Thursdays. Now it's like a little countdown, and a meltdown timer. Next week I have to do my shot. Okay this week I'm stable, next week I have to do my shot. Shit that hurts when I touch the injection site, is that bad? Internet says no. Once in awhile I want to look in the mirror. Not a whole lot, because I don't like what I see. I usually don't like what I see when I look at myself anyway, and it's compounded when I look into a mirror. Brown skin, brown eyes, brown hair, fat. Most days, I wouldn't trade being brown for the world, and some days I wouldn't want to think what it would be like to be a white straight person from a commercial, who always knew, 'Yep this is me and my body.' When I do want to look in the mirror and I do, it's different now than how I used to feel. It's becoming a stranger's face and I like that.

I don't look people in the eye, because then I imagine they see right through me. It's hard to meet my own gaze, because then I start to ask myself all these questions like, "How the hell do I explain this? Do I want to explain for the bajillionth time?"

I stay up until 5:00 a.m., most days and I don't

know why. There's this itchy feeling right in the back of my chest¬it pulls tight from my nipple straight into my heart. I stay up until I can hear my thoughts quite and buzz around. The nightmares will inevitably come when I pass out, strung high on chocolate and binge eating ice crushed at the bottom of plastic cups. I lied. I know why I stay up, and when I write it down it sounds so stupid. It sounds so fucking boring and obvious to me. You stay up late because going to sleep means you have to wake up and people have to look at you. Of course I get stressed out when my body betrays me late into the night. When you don't know who the fuck I are anymore. I just want to be me. Who the fuck is that? It's so easy to turn me into the second person you. You feel these things and not me. Who are you; that doesn't matter because it's so much easier to project into the darkness. In the dark I look into the mirror and hope that the shadows obscure my vision into who I like. When I close my eyes I can't think anymore because the thoughts going through my mind are a million little light bulbs bursting and stabbing me behind my lids.

There are a few people like me, I'd seen visible changes in one person until one day they graduated into invisibility. It intrigued me and scared me. How do you do that I wondered until I started pushing the needle into my thigh every two weeks. Clockwork. Friday 3:30 5ml circled with black pen in my planner. It all starts to feel right. I want to fall headlong into love with someone, burden them with a life of debt and insecurity. No children, no pets I write into *Craigslist*'s m4m m4w relationship ads. I look at missed connections and wonder how I've missed all these eye contacts and mutual masturbations at Flex, the gay nightclub downtown. I get curiously skeezed at all the m4t dudes looking for trans women and crossdressers to satisfy their heterosexual urges. Passable is a must apparently.

My late night broodings convince me that I will become a statistic, sex work is in my imminent future. It's not something that I'm afraid of anymore, I'm just counting the days until my diploma is in my hand and a dick is in my mouth to pay for my cozy little apartment. Will I be posting my ass all over the internet fetish sites and get on webcams to say, 'Yeah I'm a college graduate like the rest of them sweetie, ask me to tutor you.' Can I sound thirsty enough to get paid consistently for a few years? When I was younger, I didn't want to be my mother, sleeping with men to be able to live. I learned to live with it.

I don't begrudge her and I think more of her bravery every time she comes home late still. She calls me after every trick complaining that she still has to stick her leg out on the corner. I know how much truth lies in that. There is still some hope inside of me that I won't sell tail and I can be like my father. If I hadn't already changed my name maybe I'd take his title up post humerus and tell people how influential fatherhood was to me, a black teen. Instead I write poems in my journal about how I saw him on the bus again. My mom usually just stays up late with me on the phone and we watch shitty B movies until she can't stand my commentary about the stupid doctors. She usually does my shot for me when I come over every Friday, strokes my beard and clicks her teeth in a smart alec way. "Boy, don't be coming over my house with a big bushy beard no more," she warns as she gives herself her own shots of insulin and takes her rainbow assortment of pills. We compare sores from bad shots and I lay in her bed until I don't feel lonely.

I fall asleep in a fit of vertigo and sleep deprivation Tuesday night and dream that my mother is hugging me, but I'm 15 all over again. My mother rarely hugged me as a teen, so it scares me how real this feels. The comfort and happiness overwhelm me. This isn't a nightmare, but I want to wake up. The thought of my mother reaching out to me without anger or fear in her eyes makes something start up in my chest. I know that this is a dream instinctively, yet waking up seems impossible. My mother reaches down to kiss me on the forehead and I wake in a cold sweat with a scream stuck somewhere inside me. I look at my clock and it's noon, Wednesday.

I welcome the thought of going somewhere different. I slide into the second skin of flat wear and go to a meeting with my best friend at the beach. He makes my heart pitter patter even though he said he's not into me. Whenever he leans in close, I think about stupid stuff like rubbing our beards together and how I want all my clothes to smell like his cologne. My friend smiles at me with this shit-eating grin, says "Malik, you son of a slut" and we slug each other a couple times, high in spirits. I harbor a deep hatred of his boyfriend, but I can't stand the way he looks right into my eyes when we talk. I wouldn't be able to take it if we were together. We amuse ourselves at the edge of the water pretending that we will save each other from drowning if one of us falls of the pier.

I ride on the high for an hour or two on social interaction and wind down drifting through work like a robot. I methodically answer questions. When I get home and elbow my way out of my clothes I'm left with that age-old spacey feeling of being alone in the universe. I'm wondering what I'm going to do after college. Sometimes I think that I will just get a nondescript job and become a boring piece of shit forever. My name tag will make people call me Mah lick seven times a day. I gave up on actually thinking anything of myself by my second semester in college. Teaching other people how to grow up and being looked up to still warms me sometimes, but the feeling is more and more hollow. I instead read books about the infinite time you have as a child with imagination. That feeling you have when you're on the road and the world is open and inviting you to indulge in going somewhere no one knows your face. Children's adventures are the things that get me out of my funk, about leaving home about making new friends and not being afraid. Getting out of this country may be what I need, a fresh start.

It's Monday. Time for my regular. I like him, he's kind and he doesn't ask too many questions. I placed a discreet ad on *Craigslist* about a year ago and we've come to an agreement. My Thursday alarm clock has ceased to function once I stabilized on my meds. It's every week now that I insistently forget that I have to use a shit ton of medical supplies on one little shot. I just feel horny all the time now. He comes over at night and listens to my best LPs: J Dilla, Fat Jon and Michita while I finish up articles that I need to write. Then he takes me upstairs and I watch the ceiling fan, music thrumming through the walls while he holds onto my hips and grunts in time. I like this guy though. His dick pays my bills. A few more times of seeing him and I'll be out of commission for a little while. He knows why, seems sort of intrigued of the idea that I am paying bucket loads of money for happiness. You can't buy it, but you can give yourself something else to look forward to with it. I've stockpiled enough money that maybe we won't need to see each other again and I can move somewhere green like I've always wanted.

Tears sting my eyes as I strip my sheets down. I can feel the tension headache forming already. Tears don't come easily nowadays, precious resource. It's easier to imagine crying because I can rationalize my crying. I don't want to do this forever, and yet I convinced myself that I had to. I told myself that I'd end up here and made the excuses until I fulfilled my own prophecy. Glamorizing only works on children's books. My room smells stale, like all the stale things I've accumulated. All the dreams and hopes I set for myself become smaller and smaller until I rationalize never giving up what's easiest. The stale smell of two men rolling around together in a bed, of my own anxiety floating in the air. I open the window and look at my approximation of the moon, the security light higher than the rest in the neighborhood, shining right into my room and lighting it up like an underwater cave. As I shuffle my way down two flights of stairs I start to feel as if I am being submerged in overwhelmedness.

It is a sick queasy and yet calm feeling. Detached. I am disassociating, and by the time I get down to the washer, I am done with feeling sorry for myself and cycling through emotions to feel like the washing machine. The washer rocks itself through its spin cycle and I lean into its rhythm, quiet and warm.

-David Van Horn

Powa

Their eyes first met across a room full of dead bodies. Kgotso, wheeling in the last of the morgue's residents that night, noticed the security guard in the corner for the first time in what must have been six months of their working in the same building. Sthembiso stood up taller than usual, their single seeing eye locking with both of Kgotso's big brown ones. Neither of them was prepared for the fiery intensity of that gaze. Or what was to follow. With the building virtually empty and no one to witness the current of electricity between these two queer individuals but the dead of Alexandra township, they danced a silent passionate and slow waltz. Moving as though they had temporarily lost the ability to control their limbs, aware of nothing else in that semi-final resting place of death, but each other's beckoning presence. They walked towards each other.

No words were exchanged in that first meeting. Just...heat. They stared at each other, stunned by the sudden drop in each of their chests of each of their hearts. You see, this kind of thing wasn't common for those two.

Kgotso, a deaf butch lesbian isolated from most

of the world she knew, was accustomed to being invisible. She was used to having her silence silently tolerated, used to having people entirely overlook her six foot, 120kg frame, bald head, big bound chest, wide neck, hips held down by Levi's jeans when she wasn't in the pale green uniform required for her work as a wheeler of the dead at her uncle's morgue. She was accustomed to having deeper connections with dead bodies, also mute and forgotten, than with any of the live, hearing people who made up the community she'd grown up in. Once it was established that she was not only deaf, but also gay (isitabane) her family made it violently clear that they wanted nothing to do with her.

And so she'd set about her own lonely, difficult path in life, teaching herself how to communicate with her hands the way she'd seen other deaf people in the community do. She signed a unique language, an island dialect that even those in a similar disposition to hers, didn't quite know what to make of her. The few live people she engaged with daily tolerated her with curt nods as she picked out the least burst open tomatoes at the market down the road from the shack she'd built with her bare hands. They wouldn't take money directly from her, only that which she left on their table or shifty hawkers stand and when she sometimes, angrily, left without paying, the most they'd do is click their tongues in mild annoyance in her wake.

It was easier just not to see her.

It was difficult for Sthembiso not to see her. Sthembiso, who had spent the past six years prior to her employment at Mbambo's Mortuary, in prison.

Sthembiso who'd sustained a savage beating from a fellow inmate which had left their right eye completely bereft of sight and covered by a red glassy film of scar tissue. Sthembiso, who had grown up in shacks that always burned down eGomorra (the affectionate term nearly everyone used for Alex). Sthembiso who had one day woken up to find half of their body engulfed in red orange flames, their father drunkenly crawling away from the smoke, leaving the seven year old to beat the flames off with a blanket on their own. Sthembiso who had never known the human touch unless it was violent, had never known the human gaze to be without disgust or hatred. Sthembiso, who found themselves, now, moving slowly, cautiously across this cold deadly room, following the gaze and movement of Kgotso's body. They moved into an adjoining room, much smaller than the death ward, like a closet almost. The ones eyes never leaving the other's face. Once they were in the same space together, the heat between them was palpable. And so was the fear. A sharp smelling sweat rose from Sthembiso's dark black and red guard uniform, enticing Kgotso, whose nostrils flared as she moved closer to this magnetic creature before her. Sthembiso was around the same height as Kgotso, but much, much smaller, wiry, thin, long, lean and flat. Sthembiso was convinced Kgotso could hear the blood rushing through their veins. Until they noticed that Kgotso seemed to be asking them a question, nonverbally, with her eyes.

And simultaneously, Sthembiso noticed, her hands fluttered around in strange movements which were obviously some form of communication. As the realization sunk in that this was a deaf person seducing them, Sthembiso felt their knees go weak with an aching compassion for the wideness of those big brown inquiring eyes. They nodded, vigorously and clumsily beckoned for Kgotso to come towards them. Kgotso moved closer, eagerly and continued to search Sthembiso's eyes for consent, even as she drew her face so close to Sthembiso's she could inhale the warm breath from their parted lips. Sthembiso nodded again, their eye growing wide and chest constricting with desire, hands reaching out unconsciously to trace the outline of Kgotso's shoulders, chest, belly, hips. Kgotso felt herself yielding into this timid exploration of her body.

She leaned into Sthembiso's hands, allowing them to feel more of her. Sthembiso was so overwhelmed they began to tremble and it was at the sight of those first few tremors running across those long thin arms, that Kgotso planted the first gentle kiss against Sthembiso's cheek. She followed that with another search of Sthembiso's eyes. Sthembiso understood the question clearly this time, closed the lids on both of their eyes and nodded.

Their first time was swift and unceremonious. Two tall uniformed queers hunched up against a wall in a small closet room at the back of a morgue. Hands holding the other up for support even as other hot hands buried themselves down the fronts of pale green, dark red and black uniform pants. Heavy, stifled breathing, the smell of fucking quickly filling the room like the most blissful smoke. When it was over, they rested against each other for a moment. Stunned. Spent. Hungry for more. Throwing the last of their caution to the night wind of the township, they snuck out of the morgue, barely remembering to lock all doors and ignoring the curious stares of Alex's thriving nightlife. It was none of their business how people felt seeing two large bald-headed stabanes walking briskly down the road together, with eyes for nothing and no one else but one another.

Kgotso's shack was dark and freezing. She bustled inside before Sthembiso, embarrassed, stuffing discarded clothing underneath her bed, which stood on four stacks of five or six bricks in each corner, and quickly kicking her small heater on, before finding the light switch and illuminating her humble abode. Sthembiso stood in the doorway, seemingly hesitant to get in. Kgotso looked at them inquiringly. She placed her hand flat against her chest and used it to trace a circle over her chest and stomach, signing. Please? Sthembiso felt at a loss. How could they describe how oddly empowering it felt to bare witness to the sight of this home which truly belonged to someone who was clearly as much of an outcast as they were?

A home which had working electricity and no paraffin lamps or candles which would someday lead to a catastrophic fire. Kgotso beckoned for Sthembiso to come in. She bunched her fists up in front of her chest as though simulating shivering, again, signing. It's cold. Sthembiso understood this clearly and took two swift steps into the shack before closing the door behind them.

This time they were completely alone. And the fire from the first fuck still glowed beneath their brown skin. Kgotso began to undress, dropping her work pants to the floor to reveal two large ample, abundantly dimpled thighs, adorned in equal measure by golden brown stretch marks and pink-brown scars. Calves the size of oranges and a wide ass covered by large clean blue cotton panties. Her work shirt came off to reveal a white vest with a few stitches over old holes, her chest oddly flattened, her arms large and muscular, adorned at the shoulders by intricate dark blue ink tattoos. Sthembiso was a lot more reluctant to reveal themselves, afraid of the familiar rejection which always followed someone seeing their body outside of its tight casing of work or prison clothes.

Kgotso waited, trying to hide that she was shivering and giggling at the worried way Sthembiso eyed the goose flesh rising over her large thighs and arms.

Eventually the room grew warmer and Kgotso slouched comfortably, stepping out of her pants and waiting with her legs spread in a very authoritative, confident stance. Her inquiring gaze was a challenge now. Sthembiso smirked, their dark brown handsomeness deepening with the folds of skin which crinkled around their thin lips. They too began with the pants, sliding them down the dark skinned, thin, but strong thighs. They too had their own leg scars to bear. Except theirs were the mottled flesh of burned skin, a disfigurement they had been ashamed of their entire life. The removal of their work jersey and black shirt, folded carefully at their feet, revealed more of the same kind of scarring across most of their upper body which was naked. Kgotso sucked her breath in excitedly at the sight of Sthembiso's flat chest, with two neat thin scars outlining the contours of beautifully crafted chest. Thoughts raced through her mind about how it would be wonderful to have similar work done to her own ample breasts.

Stembiso wore a pair of dark green BVD's, boxer shorts and sported their own array of prison ink across their back and shoulders. The yellow-tinged light overhead cast a curious glow over the two powerful bodies towering above the contents of that tiny room. Sthembiso was the first to remove their underwear, baring a lush and dark pussy covered in grey speckled hair and a tight, toned behind. They stood casually in front of Kgotso, as though their nakedness suddenly wasn't a big deal anymore and Kgotso reached out and gently traced a finger over some of the scar tissue covering Sthembiso's left hip. Sthembiso stifled a flinch and stared defiantly at their lover. Kgotso bent down and kissed one of the neat thin scars across Sthembiso's chest and they responded by roughly pulling the other butch against them in a fierce embrace.

What ensued was nothing short of literal power. The two strong, old, butch bodies beaten and resilient yielding, opening, blossoming for the first time in lorde knows how many decades. It was power that carried them into orgasm after orgasm. Power which flowed through their steady exploration and examination of each other's tough-skinned disfigurement, broken and mended flesh showing stories of battle and survival, hard-earned masculinity and strength which just as easily gave way to gentleness and wide-eyed softness. Sthembiso whispering promises against the flesh of Kgotso's back to learn the language of hands...Kgotso using her fingers against the scarred flesh of her lover's hardened thighs, to promise never to overlook that brutal beauty. Each of them vowing, with every thrust of their forty-something year old life-worn fingers, to allow this newfound passion to serve as fuel for the rest of their days.

Around them Gomorra slept more soundly than the dead.

They woke up before the last of the smoke from the many fires of the night had billowed away. Buoyed by the unfamiliar feeling of being enfolded in warm naked flesh all through the night, they cast sweet smiles at each other and kissed, with tongue, before bounding out of bed. Each of them had dreamt of all the work which needed to be done to integrate their lives, for the bond between them to be as indestructible as the electricity which powered the entire city of Johannesburg. Kgotso thought about convincing Sthembiso to pack their belongings and come and live with her, at least until they had enough material to build a home of their own, together. Or better yet, they could use the money she had saved to apply for one of the houses the government was building for the people of Alex.

Sthembiso, pretending to be asleep, had wondered where they would be able to find some pen and paper in order to ask their sweet butch lover where the language of the hands could be learned. She had always been proud of the gracefulness of their long-fingered dark hands and gestured wildly whenever they spoke, back in the day when there were friends to speak to. Before prison. Before their hands were responsible for taking the life of another. The person responsible for the blindness of their right eye.

Sthembiso would be happy for the chance to restore gracefulness and kindness into those hands again. To restore the poetic beauty ancient lovers would commend them on, in the days when "lesbian" was a word which encompassed at least some of the complexity of who they were.

While Kgotso heated some water in an old white kettle and brought out a dark green plastic dish for them to bathe in, Sthembiso began a one-eyed exploration of the home they had spent the night in. Wondering what it would be like to have a safe place in which to go to sleep. A place which didn't double as a place of employment in the morning. Sthembiso felt this dish bath they were about to have with Kgotso was far more luxurious than any prison shower or the bath tub at the morgue in which the dead were cleansed before their loved ones came to collect them. They bathed each other, carefully caressing soapsuds over scarred brown flesh, eyes locked into each other once again.

Kgotso, preempted the slight barrier in communication and placed a pen and paper onto the bed next to Sthembiso as they pulled their work pants over legs freshly lathered with Vaseline cocoa butter.

Sthembiso paused before buttoning their pants to write in a careful block letter handwriting:

I WANT 2 LEARN HAND LANGUAGE?

And when Kgotso read their words, she squealed in excitement, nodding and snatching up the pen and paper and scribbling in her less refined handwriting:

I will teach you! But first let us go to your house and fetch your things! I want you to live with me! I have never felt like this be4.

186

Tears sprung up in Sthembiso's eyes as they read the words Kgotso had written on the page. Kgotso held the pen and paper out to them, and Sthembiso reluctantly took them from her. Kgotso was wearing a fresh pair of red cotton panties and pulling a small sports bra over her ample breasts instantly giving them the appearance of being flat against her chest. She stopped dressing when she noticed Sthembiso hadn't written anything else on the piece of paper and nudged them with her arm, before shrugging questioningly. Sthembiso wiped at their wet eyes and tried to steady their trembling hand as they wrote:

I LIVE AT MORTUARY. BATH THERE. SLEEP THERE. 2 OLD TO TRY BUILD MKHUKHU. I

Kgotso's eyes encouraged them to carry on.

SORRY.

Sthembiso could write nothing more. Kgotso threw an arm around her partner's lean muscular shoulders and squeezed. It was the first time she had hugged someone in decades and Sthembiso's hesitance in relaxing into the embrace, told her that they were just as unaccustomed to hugs as she was. Kgotso turned around so that she and Sthembiso were facing each other on the bed. She put up her right hand, with her index finger pointing up and swung that hand from her right shoulder to her left, we, then she rapidly sign-spelled the words will build a home together. Sthembiso watched her in earnest concentration, trying to make sense of the fast-paced movement of the short-fingered light brown hands. Kgotso grabbed the piece of paper and wrote:

We will build a home together. Don't worry, I will teach you

187

Sthembiso imitated the first movement they had seen Kgotso make, swinging their right hand from one shoulder to the next, in a semi circle. They mouthed the word; we. Kgotso nodded excitedly and chuckled in a rich deep voice. Sthembiso smiled when they caught sight for the first time of the gold teeth on other side of Kgotso's tiny incisors. They grabbed the piece of paper and blue pen and wrote, simply:

I LOVE YOU.

The first time either of them had ever read signed seen written or heard those three words strung together in sentence directed at them.

When they stepped out into the morning, Gomorra seemed unaware of what had transpired in the small shack in 6th street, ko6. Unaware that a formidable force had come to fruition. Joining the seemingly contradictory worlds of faces as hardened as any of the many mjita who filled the street, smoking Styvesant cigarettes, downing brown bottles of Black Label beers and tenderness buried deep inside of them, but never losing its urgent yearning for release. A few looked upon them with a bored curiosity. Another pair of izitabane strange gay women, who would have to be careful not to try get with anyone else's girlfriends. Would they have been astonished to learn that these two butches had no intention of "getting" with anyone else but each other? Would they recognize the completion of power in the union between the two? A power that was about a lot more than just muscles or tallness or tattoos. A power that was about connection, compassion, deliberate and loving communication and the might of love between two warrior folks.

They didn't hold hands or even look at each other

walking down the streets filled with stores tumbling onto the roads, shack doors opening directly into traffic, children playing half-naked and bathed in only sunlight in between stalling cars. They walked amongst their people, for the first time, feeling that they were not only home, but that they were royalty finally returned to their unruly quingdom.

*glossary

Gomorra - a name Alexandra township in the east of Johannesburg, South Africa, is sometimes called by its residents
Mjita - Men/Boys/Dudes in township slang
Mkhuku - Shack
Stabane/Izitabane - term used to describe anyone who is gay or lesbian or queer/gender-non-conforming

-Thokozane Minah

Traitor/Happy Ending

Butch bois who love deeply and keep our centers untouched… we are coyotes running wild. In our generous nostalgia, we are fucking and delighting beyond the understanding of other, softer bodies. We bring you, follow you, sniff your scent and give our muscles over to your rise and release. We come over and over in our minds: Late at night alone, we drench our hands with quiet desire and keep ourselves a fine, cellar-stained reserve. We are time-weathered stone.

The other side:

I do not like my own smell. My center is a lifeless, salted sea. I am afraid of everything. This is sometimes lonely, other times, convenient. Most times, safe. With a broad back and a low register¬-- this is how I keep my floating entrails together.

Butch bois, I can confess now: sometimes in the thick of night I imagine spilling open like water. I imagine being touched and I wake up raging with fullness. Blessed are the lovers who soak up my body and wash me ashore; who collect my moans in seashells; kiss them with curved lips and let them float onward; who know that even stones are carved by water. Lovers who take carefully and understand how to replace. I am not like them.

This is how *I* love.
Every second
betrothed to your pleasure
holding the crash of salt and sea in my veins.

-M. Willis

Movement

Questions and Answers

Abena, are you Ghanaian?

After I touched ground at Kotoka International Airport into the brown sprawling mess
that is the city of Accra, and until I stepped into the New York snow outside of John F. Kennedy International Airport four months later, I was asked a few questions on a semi-regular basis.

My father, Kwame, was born in Kumasi, Ghana, a small city in the center of a small country. Ghanaians call it the Garden City. I offer this fact to anyone who asks me what I am and if that part of me happens to be Ghanaian.

Abena is a Ghanaian name—meant for those Ghanaian girls born on Tuesdays—and I do suppose I have some Ghanaian features. Ghanaians also had a tendency to ask for my Christian name or my British name, upon discovering that my name is a traditional one. This seems to me to be awfully, perversely peculiar, as if having a Ghanaian name is not enough. ("But… your Christian name? Is it Abigail?")

Sometimes I feel like I live on the shores of a warring ocean, and sometimes I believe
firmly in the need to not prepare for certain things. So,

yes, I am Ghanaian. But when I look in the mirror, I often see a wry smile and my mother's Haitian cheekbones. My mother, Danielle, is from a small village town in the Central Department of Haiti called Saut D'eau. Saut D'eau is the French word for waterfall. In my youngest memories, my mother's village smells and sounds and looks something like the washed-out edges of old photographs: a scruffy-faced goat tied to a iron stake in my great-uncle's backyard; a brown river that flows up to my chubby arms; my great-grandmother's paper-thin brown skin; a great massive waterfall on the edge of town, shooting wet confetti rain into the palm and pitch-apple trees below; a dog with fat ticks, panting on the porch of a pink stucco ranch house; darkness and latrines and spiders.

Haiti is washed-out, although it breathes solidly in the family I have in New York, my mother and grandmother and aunts and cousins, than the Ghanaian family I went to find in West Africa. Haiti breathes in the green mangoes and keneps and canisters of rum that my grandmother smuggles into LaGuardia Airport, by way of Miami International, but it also breathes on the coasts of West Africa, in Ghana and Togo and Benin, in the high-ceilinged walls of slave castles like Elmina and Cape Coast.

I don't think it occurred to me that there was anything to know about my Haitian family in New York. Holidays, birthdays, and barbecues were always full to bursting with my mother's chattering extended—Grandma Denise; Uncles Eddie (with the dreadlocks) and Joe Aunts Juneau, Marie, and Rosemay; cousins William (the Jehovah's Witness), Yamiley, Jean, Andy, Jackie, Dennis, Cecile, and now baby Antonio (whom I have yet to meet). Grandma's apartment on Dean Street was the site of all meet and greets for the Registres: whenever a parent was stuck at work or going on vacation or exterminating rats or roaches, their children were dutifully deposited on Grandma's doorstep in Crown Heights. I remember pieces of the 20-minute drive that we would take from our home in northeastern Queens to Grandma's building. Brooklyn. In particular I remember the cemetery we would drive through, whose expanses hugged the edges of the narrow Jackie Robinson Parkway, and through which I would hold my breath and count to 12. After tumbling out of the car at Grandma's stoop, we would proceed walk up the four flights of winding projects stairs, my brother Kwame pushing and prodding me up along the way, and I would smile broadly when I reached Grandma's landing.

"Hi Gramma!"

"Hi, Grandpa!" A mischievous smile from the family matriarch.

"Aw, Gramma! You know I'm not Grandpa!"

And she would smile, and I would smell the griot and bouillon and black-eyed peas burning on her silver-polished stovetop. Grandma Denise has since moved to Elmont, a small, quiet, mostly-black suburb on Long Island. We still do the "Gramma-Grandpa" schtick from time to time, but I have never known either of my paternal grandparents. In fact, the only member of my father's extended family that I was ever close with was his brother, Apraku. Or his half-brother, as I discovered a few months ago.

My Ghanaian family has always been a mystery,

and so few of them lived in the United States at all. Indeed, the fact of my being Ghanaian never seemed to exist outside of odd symbols when I was growing up: a too-small skirt made of traditional Kente cloth that I received from "a relative" (always a relative) when I was six; the steaming tray of jollof rice that I brought to my elementary school's International Luncheon in the fifth grade; my name. I often wonder if the size of my mother's Haitian family isolated my lonely father more, if the sight of the 12 Registres around the Thanksgiving table hurt him any. By the time I was old enough to ask, my father was no longer there to tell.

My mother and father separated before I turned ten, and when my parents broke apart, I listened to shards and scraps of their arguments and heard what is best and worst about myself. That Haitians were just stupid enough to have been shipped across the Atlantic, that Ghanaians are too black African. In the current political landscape of my life, my father is prone to ignoring the Haitian flags and rainbow banners that paper the walls of my bedroom. He also has a certain proclivity for such acerbic non-sequiturs as, "Haitians are losers," and "How were your trips to the slave castles? You know you don't have any slave ancestors." At times like these, I am torn between an acid that comes from a failed marriage, and internalizing harmful ideas about half of myself. At times like these, I am often caught for a loop as to how, exactly, to be.

* * *

Abena, have you been to see your family in Kumasi?

From August to December of last year, I lived in Ghana and spent most of my time
avoiding the half of my family that lives there. I saw my father's face everywhere on the streets of Accra, saw his dark skin, his shiny bald forehead, his anger. Saw my own dark face mirrored in the thousands of rich, poor, young, and old Ghanaians who surrounded me. We visited the Wli Waterfalls in November, and while everyone waded to their necks in the cold salty water, I hung back and felt myself fly to plateaus and stucco in the Caribbean. In many ways, Haitian is the only way I know how to be. When I think of Haiti, I think of my mother and of safety and warmth, perhaps in an extremely infantile way, but as soon as I got to Ghana, I needed to be Ghanaian for everybody—my white friends looked to me for some harmless combination of authentic African tour guide and token black friend, while my African-American friends glared on with jealousy, that I was able to come to this country and find, quite literally, what they could only symbolically seek: roots.

* * *

The drifting Haiti of my memories seems especially muddy, especially hard to pin down, when remembered in tandem the crystal-clear images—in my memory and in my iPhoto album—of my semester abroad: my memory seems to be working overdrive, in snapshots of bus rides and conversations recalled verbatim.

For example, my cousin Jeffrey (Amoakohene is

199

his Ghanaian name) called me almost daily to ask how I was doing. He was born in Kumasi, like most of my family, but lived and worked in Tema, another coastal city just east of Accra. One night, after much fretting on my part, we had dinner at Labone Coffee Shop, and he brought me Ghanaian chocolate and a Kente cloth dress. I accepted the gifts, tugging uncomfortably at the collar of my button-down shirt and trying to smooth my jeans. The dress would spend the next few months folded-up in the back of my closet. "I'll save it for Amma," I reasoned, thinking of my small sister. "She's appropriately feminine." I constantly received phone calls from unknown numbers in Ghana, family members who were in Accra for the weekend and who wanted to catch a glimpse of rich Uncle Kwame's American daughter. Every time I thought to pick up the phone, I thought of the conflicted look on Jeffrey's face: one part familial love for his cousin Abena, one part disappointment (did I imagine it?) at her lack of boyfriend, lack of husband. I may have imagined all of it, but I felt this most acutely when the NYU-Accra program took us on a day trip to Kumasi:

At 4:00 in the morning on a wet-smelling October Sunday, it was already hotter than any October day in New York. Our four Resident Assistants were running in circles around the 32 kids who made up NYU's Accra program—waking and re-waking us, distributing two-liter bottles of Voltic water and Styrofoam rectangles filled with fried chicken and jollof rice. Many miles and many hours later—during which we had paid 20 Ghana pesewas (about 12 cents) for toilet paper, and took pictures with ostriches at the largest tilapia farm in West Africa—I had my headphones on, face pressed to the warm glass of our tour bus.

"Alright everyone," sang a convivial, maternal voice from the front of the bus. My sleeping classmates stirred; Julian snorted loudly and fell forward with a start. "I know it's been a long ride, but we're finally in Kumasi." The voice belonged to Christa, the Assistant Director on our campus and an American ex-pat from Philadelphia. I fished through my gray traveler's backpack, trying not to kick the empty bottles of water, now caked in mud, which lined the bottom of the bus. It was close to 3:00 in the afternoon, and I was in Kumasi.

"Hey Abby, what are you thinking about?"

I must have looked strange. I sat up and turned toward the friend who asked me.

"Nothing much. I can't believe how long it took to get here!"

"Yeah... Hey, isn't this where your dad's family is from?"

"Mm... Yeah. I guess?"

I turned around, back toward the picture windows of the tour bus, at the houses and streets and colors and children playing on dirt roads, and I imagined whole other lives for myself, outside of Queens and New York and an immigrant's America. Piles of trash burned in black plumes, shoeless kids in football jerseys roasted goats and I, who had not been back to Haiti in more than a decade, felt as though I could have been in the back of a pickup truck in Saut D'eau.

They are not so different.

"But," I thought to myself, very deliberately. "This isn't Haiti, I was six the last time I was there.

This is Kumasi, and I am 20 and a college student and a lesbian in a country where to be so is illegal."

I turned off my phone and turned up my music.

* * *

Abena, do you have a boyfriend?

The week before I boarded a plane to Anglophone West Africa was suffocatingly hot, and I had put off all of my packing for the three days before takeoff. One evening, as cicadas buzzed lazily in the maple tree outside my bedroom window, my father interrupted my haphazard packing spree in order to impart a particular bit of wisdom in me.

"You know I have always accepted you, Abena."

"Mmhmmm," I intoned. I bit my tongue, bent over my dresser and examining two nearly-identical pairs of pants. I was trying to decide exactly what shade of blue would best complement my new African personality.

"Sit down and talk with me."

My father has a very peculiar way of talking about my sexuality, and it is one that involves never actually saying the word "gay." But, in very roundabout and awkward terms, we proceeded to discuss my sexual orientation, my fierce love for the New York City Pride Parade, my tendency to gravitate towards activism in issues of gender and sexuality.

However, my father warned, my sexuality was not something that I was to discuss in any context in Ghana. "I am only concerned for your safety," he implored. I knew what he meant; I had done some casual Googling, had read the articles that friends and

202

acquaintances were circling on various social networking sites. *Ghana Orders the Arrest of All Homosexuals. Ghana Cracks Down on Gays*. And here sat my father, my absentee father, sitting on my twin mattress and telling me: stay in the closet because I love you. Since coming out to my father in late high school, it has always seemed as though he accepts, or at least tolerates me. But something in his voice told me that my Ghanaian family, the family I never met and never knew, would not. "And in any case," he said with an air of finality. "It is not proper to talk about such things with family."

Ah. So, there I was, standing at the precipice of twin mountain peaks called Your Father and Your Past, and a shove called Homophobia sent me tumbling back into the abyss. I could not be both Ghanaian and gay, my father was telling me, so I decided I had to choose. I chose gay.

I was never and cannot imagine being asked if I am attracted to women while I was in Ghana, but once, while conducting some interviews on the street for a project I was completing on the queer community's presence in Ghanaian media, a man stood with me behind the camera, and spoke candidly with his friend about the good uses of rape as a tool for curing lesbianism.

I also don't usually feel guilty for my more masculine-of-center gender expression. Fairly recently, however, I was walking through the men's section of Macy's, riffling through flannel shirts and track jackets. It was a few days before Christmas, and a few days after I landed back in New York. I felt explicitly out of place, gendered in a way that I have never felt in New York City. I seemed to feel the gaze of my Ghanaian family, who would have been so happy to see me, in Kumasi and in a Kente dress.

"We just want to see you!" the voicemails and messages and emails said.

Experiencing Ghana for the first time as an adult was very different from experiencing Haiti as a child. "Do you want to run through the waterfall?" becomes "Do you have a boyfriend?" Your age conflates with your status as family member and woman, into a list of heteronormative assumptions that bury your existence as a person.

I am at a point in my life where there is something in the thought of speaking with my family that gives me panic attacks, and all of this has grown into a wedge between me and my ancestors and ancestry.

* * *

Abena, wo te Twi?

Abena, you speak Twi?

Twi is a principal indigenous language in Ghana, and the most commonly-spoken language in Accra. It is also a language that I heard a bit of growing up; sometimes my father would answer the phone and lapse into a string of garbled sounds I could not understand, and I imagined him sharing secrets I would never hear with people I would never meet. I do not speak Twi, but I do understand bits and pieces of the very musical Haitian Creole language. When I was five, my babysitter's name was Madame Apollon, and at breakfast every morning, the two of us could be seen giggling and throwing cereal at my big brother Kwame, all the while chattering away in Creole.

"Bonjour, Madame!"

"Bonjour, Abby! Ça va?"

"Ça va bien!"

"Cafe au lait, Abby?"

"Non non! Du jus, s'il vous plaît, Madame!"

I often found that people in Ghana—saleswomen arranging oranges at the market, men playing mancala on the street—were grossly offended by my inability to speak Twi. I found myself longing to respond, "No, but I do speak Creole," or "No, but why you could always ask my dad why he never taught me." My resentment towards my father for not teaching me Twi is naive and self-centered, to be sure. After all, what do I know of the immigrant's imagination, of wanting your child to be normal and American and to assimilate?

After living in Ghana for four months, 120 days, I do know how to say a few words in Twi. Allo. Hey, friend. Yebeyhia bio. See you soon. And one more little thing. On sticky hot Accra mornings, whenever I walked through the house gates on the way to Creative Writing or African Popular Music, the guards would smile and say something very curious. It wasn't a question.

Abena, ko bra.

Abena, go and come.

"Go and come" is the very particularly Ghanaian way of saying something like, come home safely, because I care about you. So, to Ghana and to Haiti and to my absentee Ghanaian roots, and to all of these other slippery questions from last semester, I would like to answer:

* * *

Alright, Ghana. I was not always comfortable. But for now I am safe, and I will try to go and come. Hopefully, I'll be able to answer these questions a little more honestly when I do.

-Abena Opam

The House I Live In

Tell me how to get home. Tell me how to get home when I feel a vacant lot, an open scab, a wound where home once was. Tell me how to get home when I am a mosaic of places, and all I have are postcard memories.

You know, I was born a Sagittarius. and I didn't think that meant anything until my partner told me that sagittarius is a wanderer. And when my mother was pregnant with me, she would commute everyday over two trains from New Jersey to Queens. somehow it seems to be ingrained in me, this longing, this tendency, towards always wandering. Towards always moving. Towards what I don't know. I just wanna go. I want to see. I know there is more to this world than where I am right now.

That's what I said in 2007 when I was 17 and wanted to leave New Jersey. I came from the segregated lower-income immigrant side of a "diverse" town in northern New Jersey. I came from the Catholic church side of town. My butchness is wrapped in my race and class and my Filipino working-class upbringing; of apartments in multifamily houses, balikbayan boxes, and rosary novenas before Christmas.

I knew I had to leave. Because the kind of butch I am is Bruce Springsteen. I wear New Jersey like a badge, like it's a heart on my leather jacket sleeve. Like, baby we were born to run. Now that I find myself on the other side of that segregation line in downtown well-to-do Boston, I cannot let myself get too comfortable in upper-middle-class "perfection."

Don't get me wrong. I like Boston. but I'm not at home.

I've recently realized that part of my dislike for downtown Boston also stems from this class difference. My father has worked a variety of blue-collar jobs and my mother was an ESL instructor. Although my mother attended university in the Philippines, I was the first person in my immediate family to finish college in the U.S. (thanks to some generous financial aid). Now I am in Boston, in a hub of intellectual institutions and white-collar jobs. I've finished my masters at an ivy league (again thanks to some very generous financial aid, which at the same time still leaves me with loads of debt). I have my dream job, which lets me work in labor history—but it still doesn't feel totally right.

I mean, it all happened so quick, sometimes I feel like I am barely catching up with all this. I take a look around me, and then like I've got whiplash in a car crash: how did this even happen?

No one gives you a map for class mobility. and I don't mean to sound like a privileged person complaining about their privilege. I truly don't. I don't feel too great about often being one of the few not-exactly-white persons on the Green Line. I am also 100% not down with gentrification. I don't wanna be a gentrifying force by moving into an area with more folks of color, when I look more white than Asian-American.

I can hear the back of my head saying, no one gives you a map, kid. But I just wanna go home. I just wanna feel right somewhere.

* * *

This butch emerged from the determination to go and see.
Now, I don't know what "masculine" or "feminine" traits are, honestly
and I don't exactly feel of-center-anything,
but spunk and determination are really the only things I consider fitting
for the butch in me.

Spunk and determination
to go beyond expectations,
to leave and learn and see
    but to wear New Jersey like a badge, on my sleeve.

I am curious,
I still want to go where I can and see what's around
but I also still feel the pull
the want to feel right somewhere.

* * *

where did I get my map?
trains run, remember?
    and veins run too.

bklyn boihood

my map is constructed
by various train lines
and tracks that I've jumped,
    all of which
carry blood
straight to the heart.

and while all these different places are a part
of me there's still something missing,
maybe —
    like I haven't found the perfect place yet
or maybe that perfect place
doesn't exist

    is there a somewhere
    in between
    the PATH train, the subway
    the amtrak, the T?

maybe I should just learn to get comfortable
with making my home my body,
with carrying it, everywhere, on my back.

because:
dontcha know kid,
no one's gonna give you a map

    maybe the mysterious somewhere
    is somewhere underneath my skin:
    somewhere, someday
    I will own this house I live in.

but for now, home looks like the stars on a clear, still
night
when I feel small, and in awe,
and the whole world is surrounding me.....

I suppose home is something
I'll learn to carry with me.
>   (you know, I always thought snails were
>   endearing for some reason.)

home is
my butch sense
of determination:

it starts with leaving,
and getting to see

(home is something I live in, and I carry it with me.)

-Resi Polixa

Masculinity as Phantasmagoria

"you are my shelter from the storm/and the storm/ my
anchor/ and the troubled sea"
-evie shockley, "ode to my blackness"

I. shelter from the storm; anchor

The TSA agents don't know what to do with me. In
airports, I'm always checked at least twice. I've come
to like this game, to find humor in its absurdity. First,
my hair. The older woman TSA agent puts on rubber
gloves the way a urologist might when examining
male genitalia. She pats down the top of my dreads,
then lifts up the back of my hair and feels my
shoulders, the base of my neck. Then, the older man
TSA agent steps in.

"What is your last name?", he says. Here, they
want to see how my voice sounds, it doesn't really
matter what my last name is, all that matters is what
timbre comes out. In this particular incident it is March
and I'm getting over a cold. My voice is a bit gruff and
deeper than usual. When addressing strangers though, I
deepen my voice. That's just what it is.

"Johnson," I reply.

Both agents look at each other, then at me in the style of Three Stooges-era slapstick comedy. "… and your first name?" the woman is thoroughly confused. Here, they want to know if my first name denotes a gender; if I am perhaps an Ann, Rebecca, Jessica, or maybe a Benjamin, Phillip, Robert.

"Taylor," a smug look comes across my face. Not the answer they hoped for. I've always been proud of my name for its indecisiveness, it's staunchly ungendered nature. This is the point when the TSA agents must decide which one of them will pat me down. The man moves closer to me.

"I'm going to pat you down now…" his voice gives in on the last word, a slight inflection like maybe he meant to say it as a question but wants to seem certain in his decision.

"Ok."

There is something to be said here about security and freedom and fear and physical contact with strangers in America, but that will come later. This part is about happiness, about feeling secure in falling out of gender.

* * *

It's ok to make it up. At nine, I was not the smoothest. My version of masculinity was fantastic, not in the sense of perfection, but in the sense of wild and extravagant. I opened doors for all my girl classmates, and sometimes the boys too. I was extremely polite. At my friend's tenth birthday party, her mom, Ms. Henderson, gave us all candy apples. I didn't care much for them, but I do take one in this insistence because it is polite, because

213

I've thought about kissing her, because I want her to keep thinking that I'm a boy.

"Are you having fun?" I mumble awkwardly in the kitchen, when all of my friends leave. "Of course!" she is so forgiving. "Are you having fun?" she points a shiny, caramel-dipped apple in my direction. I oblige, and hope one of my friends' will eat it in my stead. I pass behind Ms. Henderson, who is facing the stove, my right hand grazes the top of her ass just below her hips.

"I'm having a great time", I reply confidently.

* * *

The Black man around my age who picks me up from the car service app on my phone assumes that I too am a man. He disarms himself, asks me a simple question. "Who do you listen to?", he begins "D'Angelo…" only part of my response, but I get it out and let him continue. My masculinity makes room, even for other boys.

"In New York, you always gotta be hard, see I'm from Carnarsie. We don't play, can't really be in touch with my feelings, you dig. But, you cool son. Mad chill. But y'all do got pretty women down here though, for real. Oh, I know, you get mad girls, huh? Yea, you is a pretty nigga".

Indeed.

II. storm and troubled sea

Picture my limbs, spry and brown. Arms akimbo at my side. In front of the mirror, fearing my body had betrayed me. My body as grotesque specimen, exceeding its borders. I knew how to be kind, to be

214

soft in my interactions, but not how to welcome that softness from myself. In an attempt to remain in boyhood, I began hunching my shoulders, rounding them a bit so that my chest became barrel-like, and not so present. Here, I needed to figure out my body. I would layer T-shirts on T-shirts to give myself a flat chest, but it wasn't a lasting solution. Masculinity means patience with self.

When there are nine guns drawn on you, you have to be very still. I think of Sakia Gunn, Trayvon Martin, Ramarley Graham, Sean Bell, Oscar Grant. The names cycle through my head like a rolodex, a mantra. I forget my own name, they don't ask for it. Most young kings get their head cut off, right?

Last July, I began binding my chest. Binding in the summer can be an arduous task. The body with all its sweat and expansion in the heat, is unforgiving even to Velcro and elastic. However, after an hour struggle trying to fit this new shield across my chest, I stood in the mirror, arms akimbo, marveling at what a boy I'd become, how thankful I feel to have "made it myself". Who did I see to be except myself? That same day, I watched a courtroom in Florida succumb to the obsession of Black pathology, the acceptance of the inevitable death of Black masculinities by the state (read: White supremacy). My masculinity is impractical.

In Tribeca, I have nine guns pointed at my body. The guns all have faces. If I yell, then the guns will yell back. I don't make any quick moves.

"I have the keys," I say directly to the Black cop who keeps yelling. "Where are you from? You don't belong here? You got guns? Where's the weed? What

215

did you steal?", he gets closer to me, leading with his gun: "You tough, nigga?"

What I know is how to move through the world like smoke, how to hold my head and my hands, how to wear my skin like an armor.

"I'm going to go into my pocket and get the keys, then I'll take you to the fifth floor," I speak to the cops as if I'm part of a Hooked on Phonics instruction video. It's an apt methodology. All ten cops get in the elevator with me. "Hurry up nigga," the Black cop wants to make sure I know that he still has his gun drawn. On the fifth floor, I open the door to my white ex-girlfriend's apartment.

"You know these people?" one of the white guns speaks up.

In the hallway I hear one of the other white guns talking with the woman who summoned them all. "Well, I've just never seen him before, and I saw him in the window, and, well, I just wasn't sure," she squeaks out, sensing the error in her ways. Weeks later the woman who called the guns on me will write me on an index card and send flowers, as if it was a funeral: "Please accept my sincere apologies for the trauma I caused you".

What I've got is a set of impossible bones.

-T. Johnson

Low Visibility

In the morning, our plane began to curl downward like a rebellious strand of hair gone straight. I looked out over the cloudscape, a heavy swell of shadows that had been sucked up into the sky, swirling with the corals and blues of the sunrise, and wondered about the other side of turbulence.

Having passed through the dysphoria of landing, where your belly's lost in some buoyant limbo, what would touchdown finally feel like? I wanted to skip alla that. I wanted to be someone, somewhere ¬ clearly defined. I was on the heels of another runaway attempt, this time from a turbulent coming out as a transguy in my new hood of North Philly, where I was called faggot by neighbors and random streetdudes on the daily. I'd been flirting with IDing as genderqueer for a while before coming to the conclusion that I was surely and truly a guy and needed to be read as such. But the process of transitioning got so traumatic that I just dropped it all and ran.

A week after selling all my shit on *Craigslist*, I boarded a plane to my mother's native Ecuador, hoping I'd fly off into a new skin of set identity. Time don't stop. But at my tío's house in Ecuador, it ticked along like a broken metronome, dragged like a costeño's Spanish. My first night in Guayaquil stretched out in a sweaty warp of panicked thoughts that reeled through my head in slow-mo loops: what the fuck am I doing here? The cheap colchón sunk beneath my body hammock-like and tiny bichos tracked constellations across my skin for hours as I tried to come to grips with my new reality. The one where my dumbass inertia got me running right onto center stage of The Closet: Third World Edition. After everything I'd gone through in the States to be recognized as male, here I was, meeting my Ecuadorian family for the first time, who had been watching me grow up via photos abuelita carried with her on her visits back. They expected a niña and instead, got me.

Gender roles are strict in Ecuador and I could see in their expressions that I stuck out like something out of sci-fi, hairy legged, bald-headed, tattooed and pierced, but I was hoping they'd love me anyway. I was so eager for acceptance that I forgot to rehearse for the inevitable boyfriend questions. My tías would corner me in their chipped concrete kitchens that reeked of cat piss and good food, and demand—¿y tu novio? I'd always get mad surprised when they asked. I still do. How could anyone read me as straight? I'd been dealing with homophobia and misgendering ever since I was an adolescent tomboy—even my teachers got a kick out of fucking with me. This was the first time in my life that I'd summoned the guts to do anything about it, to reclaim some agency over my own story. But here my fam was, stealing all my thunder. I was hoping my complete lack of a gender presentation would answer the novio interrogations for me.

While I wasn't butch enough for the queers back in the States, in Ecuador, I was read as 100% marimacho, 100% of the time. But the talk of Ecuadorian families is laced with bullshit, and we do not discuss esas cosas. We pretend. You'll find one, mija, they promised. Performing gender fluidity in Ecuador was often a question of safety, but presenting as masculine of-center never felt like a choice. I realized my new default gender was female again, but I wasn't ready to grow my hair hip-length and bind it in trenzas like the other indígenas, neither. No dresses, no makeup, nada de eso, plis. I was afraid of being too visible but struggled at the same time with desiring, desperately, to be seen.

The struggle played out in Guayaquil's bus terminal where I quietly agonized on which way to pee. My too-big backpack pressed me closer to the ground and the barenaked fluorescent lights made every line in my face and each bead of sweat all the more visible as my hunched my way to the toilet. I left that arid room at my fam's place behind and began backpacking around South America but freaked out in the bathroom before even boarding the first bus. In the stall, I'd reflexively reached for the plastic tube that helped me to pee standing up, but quickly dropped it and turned right back around, afraid that someone would see me facing the wrong way and alert the media or something. I imagined armed guards busting down the door, arresting me mid-piss and drafting me off to one of the notorious lesbian "conversion" camps set up by the country's evangelicals. I gave up and squatted.

Finally walking over to board the bus, I passed a

driver who took one look at me and said, "Women don't look any different than men these days," drawing laughter from his friends. On the road, I started getting used to it. Hell, the States had given me years to prepare. Men muttering "marimacho" when I walked down cobbled streets alone at night, men yelling "maricón!" from the open window of a speeding car— one guy got up in my face and asked "Hombre, o mujer?" in the middle of a bus terminal packed with transients. Mostly, I'd just get called "señorito" by accident, but that never was no big deal. All you gotta do is wait, watch for the first light of realization to dawn on the reader's expression until they are warmed by the amusement of their own error. "Lo siento, lo siento, lo siento," they say, as they laugh.

On the road, I approached big cities with a hunger to hang around other queers and gender misfits, and I found them, but relaxed into something like solace in the remote villages, mountaintops, open deserts and rainforests I passed through, where there was less pressure to perform as anything.

From the tiny towns that dot the cordillera of the Andes to far reaches of the Caribbean peopled by few, I was relegated by locals to the finite status of an outsider, one which I readily embraced. Feeling foreign introduced me to myself again, gave me the space to explore ambiguity the same way I explored the seemingly illimitable terrain. Tenaciously. There were countless ways to be, it said. That "off" feeling I'd always felt in the pit of my belly waned the deeper I ventured into the folds of the tierra. I thought being assigned the wrong gender was the offender, and maybe that was part of it, but something clicked inside me as soon as I landed in Ecuador, como un idea that had been passed down to me through bloodlines. This shit is deeper than hombre o mujer, I realized - the forces of colonialism which ripped my family from our lands also forced us to assimilate into a rigid gender binary that I couldn't get with. I'd always felt out of place in the States because I was.

My body remembered Ecuador, like an old song, even though I'd never been there before. In the rugged cradle of the South American backcountry where the elements forced me to deal, where the current of time moved in playful waves, morphing days on the road into something BANI AMOR 4 magical, I felt the layers of identity that had been put upon me, that I'd put upon myself, dissipate. Identifying myself as one gender or another got a whole less urgent 'cause I'd begun to feel at home in my skin in a way I'd never felt anywhere else, and I let go. I didn't know where I fell on the spectrum of gender—I never had and perhaps wouldn't know for a long time ahead—but that was OK. Yes, some folks are homophobic here—gender rebels catch hell around the globe—but they aren't armed to the teeth neither and there's an aspect of respect to the culture that's severely lacking in Gringolandia. That bullshit-laced talk I so resented also works to protect me. People would rather assume you're straight and berate you with the novio questions until you got the guts to come out and say, you know what, yo soy queer. Although those aren't words I've said to my family here, yet, I haven't lied about no boyfriend neither. If they wanna pretend otherwise, that's on them. I never even came out to my family in the States ('cause I don't think any of us should have

221

to) but they know what the deal is. Gender identity is another animal I'm not gonna pretend I got figured out, but at least in Ecuador, I began feeling free to not have to, and I've found that that's what suits me.

Turbulence sucks, but landing in a place you don't belong is worse. Giving up is not usually a good thing, but it forced me to get comfortable with that nebulous space between identities, the terra incognita between colonized lands on a map, and get real with who I really was. Today, I know I'm not trans, and maybe I'm not cis, but I really don't give a shit anymore. I live openly as my truest self surrounded by supportive folks in the capital of the country, free to stand with one foot in each hemisphere and look up at the clouds floating by. They're fluid and full of chaos, but look peaceful from where I've landed.

-Bani Amor

The History Channel

My father waited until I was 18 to look me up. And then he waited another two years to make sure he was good and sober before he found me.

One afternoon he finally called my mother, using the number he'd kept from friendlier times, and asked if my brothers and I would consider meeting him. She emailed all three of us¬her signature mix of perturbed and nonchalant thrumming through¬ where we'd each scattered to our big brick-walled schools. You're legally adults now. It's your choice if you want to know him.

No, they echoed.

Yes, I said in turn. And I let my curiosity lead me to a black metal bench.

As I walked¬ not too quick, not too slow ¬towards the bus stop he and I agreed to meet at, my eyes searched for a bald head and hickory brown skin. Will he still look the same? He would, I decided. It'd only been six years since I saw him last, but it was aeons in parenting time that we both agreed, without saying, he couldn't gain back. He'd forever be some reverberation of the same man, but I'd gone from gangly pre-teen to grown adult and simply wasn't the reserved child he knew back then.

But I'm sure he realizes that. After all, he'd found me by searching on the Internet, and there wasn't a mention of me without "LGBT" trailing shortly behind. I'd been vocal as a queer woman since I'd hit my cloistered campus a couple years before. And this wasn't the occasion to tell him that I was certain I'd someday, when the timing was just right, transition to become a man. It took us years at a time, whole metamorphoses, just to gather enough resolve to share the same space; what would it take to share a gender?

Would it hit some sort of restart button, unlock a place in him we never encountered where he could actually be a father to his hijo, his son? Would that be bearable, or would it break down something inside me?

Anyway, I'd always given him inklings about my inner life in measured doses, even as a child; he knew I was a lesbian, that was enough. He said it didn't bother him with a grin, pride-widened ¬not that it mattered. I had nothing to lose that I hadn't already, and he had everything to gain.

* * *

Arriving straight from a job interview, trim hair slicked back and curves stuffed into a stiff, gray button-down, the points of my leather wingtips stuck out from khakis that caught slightly under the heels. I was short, probably hadn't gained much height since the last time I'd said "Dad" and really meant it. 5'2", just like him, and all done with sprouting. When I reached him, he stood up quickly and our eyes met on an even plane.

He hadn't aged a day. A plain white T tucked into blue jeans, his best white sneakers, the black hair fringing his bald spot cropped short. He was clean and neat, tight-bodied, just as I'd imagined. His gold tooth flashed when he beamed, and he pulled me tight to his squat frame, wrapping me in arms that bulged with familiar muscles. The same arms I remembered the clearest from childhood, so different from my mother's pale, soft ones. I'd tugged on their dark hair, traced my fingers over faded tattoos picked up in jail cells, asked him about scars from all those biking and driving accidents.

I'd dreamt, since then, of having those exact arms on my own body. Swelled, hard biceps, ropy veins curving like uncharted rivers beneath the skin, thick, square fingers rough from hard labor.

We embraced like warm acquaintances as a train rumbled the ground beneath us. I smiled genuinely, if blankly, devoid of animosity; I was devoid of most feelings towards him by now. Though he'd come and gone for the final time when I was 14, he'd never truly been a presence ¬not on my birth certificate, not on a joint custody agreement, not in my last name.

When others held me in their gazes, they could barely sense him there at all—perhaps only when the light caught right on my tan skin, brown-black hair, and chocolate-covered eyes. He was my namesake, but I carried a feminine, anglicized version; my mother's surname colonized it, and I could never follow the Spanish that used to drop from his lips like water.

No, he hadn't been there to reveal the other half of me, too busy "off drinkin'an'druggin'." My mother had named his peculiar occupation so many times, repeating the story so far back in my memory, that my child mind had made it into one long, harmlessly comical word.

As we stood together on the sidewalk, I considered he might still be dnd'ing, but his eyes were clear, his movements fluid and in control. I didn't need to find a reason to end this early. So we stood, a few paces of space between us, for several minutes, discussing a plan. As he spoke in deep tones, his eyes flitted and excitement coursed through his voice.

Memories stirred. He'd always been this jazzed, always ready for the next big thing—and he used to get me hyped too, drawn into visions of his comeback. He was going to own a cleaning business. He was going to be a nurse for Catholic priests. He was going to pick apples for a monastery. He was going to teach computer skills to Spanish-speakers. He was going to have regular visitations with my brothers and I.

And he was going to show up. He was.

Because when he was focused, he had a fire, his own self-renewing fuel cell. I always figured that's where I got my own passions from, even with the queer miles between his and mine. But when work got tough or monotonous, he'd eventually waiver and sputter, and his addictions would claim him once again.

I'd accepted that this was the way it would be early in life; my mother did too, and she'd mostly kept my brothers and I out of his wavering sightline. When I'd occasionally think about him as I grew, I moved from the rosy fantasies of my early childhood to steel visions of him in some anonymous gray cityscape, going through the same cycle, either drinking up, shooting up, or sobering up. When I thought to Google search him on my 18th birthday, I confirmed it: all that surfaced was an arrest report for disorderly conduct.

But back on the sidewalk, a new dizzy adventure was beginning in the way it always did with him: uneventfully. Low-key, but building slowly towards a peak only he could see. I weighed our first restrained minutes together and decided it was safe to sit by the pond and chat with "Dad"—I still stumbled, then called him that word for lack of a more exact one, though in a few brave moments back home I had been able toss about his first name casually.

As we strolled through back streets towards the water, we caught each other up on our time lapse in broad strokes. He'd been sober two years, was cleaning windows, honest work, and spending time at the library. He lived alone, spartan, surrounded by a few books—his favorites were spy novels, I somehow remembered—and an old TV that stayed on the History Channel. He ate outside the apartment, kept company outside the apartment. He was attending sobriety meetings regularly, just knew that the greatest thing he'd done in life was bring three beautiful children into the world.

He praised my mother for the good job she'd done raising me, and then wondered aloud if I'd let him be there for me now—do things that my mother, with her ailing body, couldn't anymore, like teaching me how to drive. He'd send me a manual, come by regularly, quiz me, drill me, lead me to a victory. He'd throw in some money to help with my rent, too. He could afford it; he really wanted to. Maybe someday he'd even help me get a car.

I nodded along, as always. Yes, sure, sure.

As long as I'd known him, his love always came down to pipedreams like this—usually of money, objects—that stood in for a physical existence, that asked, silently, for some kind of forgiveness.

We found an empty wooden bench abutting a bike path and sat, feet side-by-side in the city-sparse grass, contemplating the glinting pond before us, as if we were sailors surveying the unknown. I told him about majoring in gender studies, while falling short, as usual, of explaining what exactly that meant; I moved comfortably into describing how I'd plotted queer gatherings on campus, been trained in peer counseling. He listened attentively, ivory smile expanding with each accomplishment. When I finished, he turned and considered me with big eyes, letting out a "wow" like a slow, low whistle. We let that hang between us.

I knew you would be the one, he said then, voice warm with emotion; he was extending my list of feats. Out of the three of you, you'd be the one to let me see you. You've always been interested in history. Just like me.

I dipped my head; it was true. Though I didn't have particularly strong urges to see the whole picture of my father, there were times I'd ached to feel a connection to a blurry line of brown people who shared my blood— maybe even who looked like me. Though, I'd eventually conclude, they probably wouldn't. My skin was too watered down by whiteness. My life, poverty-shaped as it had been, too unscathed by the daily barbs of racial oppression. Humans, we're flawed and narrow-eyed¬we're built to stop short at the skin, and not X-ray through muscles, nerves, veins, to the blood.

Even if, in their hearts, that shadow family wanted to claim me, I wondered if there wouldn't always be an invisible membrane stretched taut and impermeable between us.

* * *

I have something I brought for you, Dad said slowly. He paused. I could tell he'd been holding onto this for the right moment.

Money, I thought—maybe an embarrassing amount, which would explain his unusual hesitation. I immediately decided that I'd accept it, but wouldn't let it hold the sway of a bribe.

But as he leaned down to his leather satchel and tugged, I could tell that what he sought was something thicker and heavier than a few bills or an envelope. His hands emerged, cradling a worn blue binder covered in cracking laminate. Small, spidery letters on the front read "Photo Album."

I kept these for you, for when you got older. He held the book out to me. A subconscious thought drifted to the surface, surprising me with its truth: I had never expected him to leave me something like this, something worth holding onto

Over the years, especially when I was young, my father had given me many gifts, as if a shower would cover the drought of his absences. But none were more than trinkets I held onto tightly even as I outgrew them with each passing minute. The cash was spent, the toys eventually discarded. Now, sitting on the bench, two adults shoulder to shoulder, I found him offering me a part of what my heart had been muttering about for years, now placing it carefully on my lap. We would unearth it together if I wished; we would move at my pace, as much or as little as I wanted.

Did I want to? his eyes, nearly identical to mine, asked wordlessly.

I checked myself, then committed. I flipped open its first plastic page, revealing a glossy picture of my father, ageless, standing straight-backed and chest-out at a podium, smiling and mid-sentence. He was speaking at a sobriety meeting, he explained, trying to recall when and where and how. We kept moving through photo after photo of himself, some of them polaroid-ancient, and a handful of my brothers and me as babies, then toddlers, then elementary schoolers. And then we slowed to a halt: mid-page, mid-album, the first unfamiliar face.

He tapped the faded picture. That's your cousin Daniel, he explained, scanning the friendly, oaken features. Below it lay a picture of the same young guy next to a woolly, dark-skinned old man, his aging body in an ever-so-slight proprietary lean towards the old-fashioned car to his left, button-down shirt open and stretched over a barrel-shaped torso, shiny leather shoes planted in thick, green grass.

That's my father, Dad continued, pointing. Your grandfather, in Puerto Rico. He stopped, waiting for an indication that he could keep moving on to the next page. I lingered, taking the image in.

My grandfather. I had never seen his face before. My eyes gravitated to his full head of curly white hair, his wide, flat nose and handsome, proud features, his rich brown skin several shades deeper than my father's. In America, I knew instantly he'd be lumped into the "African-American" catch-all—and with a new clarity I understood why islanders bristled at their history being flattened into one continent. I wondered, with a twinge of shame, why it hadn't occurred to me yet that my grandfather—or grandmother, for that matter—could be black; I'd even recalled reading a word for this large segment of his homeland's population. Afro-Puerto Rican.

I felt the weight of a new kind of absence, thinking a thought that I would return to again and again in the following months: if I'd passed him on the street, I wouldn't have been able to tell we were kin. Not if our lives depended on it.

* * *

I shook off my instinct to sit and brood; my father and I hadn't ever been intimate enough for me to share the depths of my longing for solid roots, though he knew that my mother was estranged from her own family— meaning, as he had surely witnessed at one point, that she, my brothers, and I had largely fused together as an unmoored, isolated unit

I moved on: I'd told myself if we reached a fresh place in our conversations, I would reveal just a bit more of a story he would want to know, if he had been able to imagine it existed. I took a breath.

I have something to share with you too, Dad. A year ago, I wanted to learn more about our family.

I recalled to him how I'd hit an existential wall: I'd gone on too long without knowing nearly anything about a past I could only see wisps of myself in. My history stopped short abruptly at him and my mother, so I figured the Internet would have to be the workaround. I had opened a profile on an ancestry website with a cautious flutter in my chest.

Records of my mother's family flourished; I'd been able to follow her line easily back to England and Ireland, and had finally stopped keeping track in the 1700's because there were just too many branches to follow. At a certain point all I could see were a wash of similar names interrupted only occasionally by quaint maiden monikers banished to obscurity by marriages to Kellaway men.

I tried to recall a time when I hadn't seen myself as part of that group of men, at least in my future projections of my manly self. A long time ago—a lifetime—I knew I had worried that my own name would be lost to history on my wedding day. The worry seemed so backwards now.

I'd switched tracks, typing in my grandfather's name—which I knew in full, since my father was his "Jr." The query returned a ghost: no solid leads. Either the records weren't available online, they'd been mangled during immigration, or they were as jumbled through colonization and bureaucratic bungling as the records of the other Puerto Rican families whose stories I encountered when I turned in desperation to the message boards. And without consulting my father, I had no way of knowing what other names were married with ours. I could only sift through hundreds of similar names and hope the date-stamps and locations hinted at something familiar.

I seethed with more curiosity about my father's family every hour that passed without clarity—now that I had allowed myself to grasp for this in earnest, I didn't want to walk away empty-handed. So I posted an anonymous message to the ancestry forum. It took a week until a stunned email landed in my inbox.

Maria had been searching fruitlessly for clues to our family too. A 40-something West coast housewife, she said her mother was my grandmother's sister—and she'd never stopped wondering about my father and his sister, who'd been dropped on her family's doorstep when they were young children. She said that my grandmother Felicia had been separated from my grandfather by then; the family's black sheep, addicted to heroin, she never returned for her children, and died an early, mysterious death.

My great aunt had had too many children of her own to care for, so she called my grandfather in Puerto Rico to come retrieve the son and daughter he barely knew. My father and aunt were left with their own grandmother on the island after their father immigrated to the US; they eventually found their way back to New York together as teenagers and encountered a robust group of half-siblings from my grandfather's subsequent marriage.

They also found their educations interrupted, their means of survival coming from the streets. They'd become addicts, too, before they knew what hit them.

How are they? Did they do okay? Maria wanted to know. He has three children? All in college? This is incredible! Yes, I'd told her. But you have to know: my mother raised us alone. My father's been in and out of rehab, jail, shelters; so has his sister. I barely even know them, and we haven't spoken in years. I can't put you two in touch. I'm sorry.

I wished I could have fulfilled her mother's

233

desire—tell her that those abandoned little kids she'd held in her heart all these years had made it through unbroken. But it simply wasn't true. I wasn't my father's daughter. I wasn't his son either. The best thing he'd done for me was bouncing off, to his next scheme or spiral, and staying far away.

Maria was sorry to hear things had turned out this way. I turned my gaze away from my hands and looked at my father's eyes, dark and wet like mud puddles: He was sorry too. For what he'd missed, and what I'd missed. For what was out of our control but still shaped us, for what couldn't be changed no matter how strong we yearned for it.

I closed the photo album and held it.

-Mitch Kellaway

Mother/\Earth

A Conversation Overheard. Between Grandparents.

They sit in armchairs three feet apart.

The same seats for 25 years. Reupholstered, never moved.

Under them rest the carpet I sat on. This place, a second home. A refuge. The soft smell of fruit trees moves through it. A place to be sent to in tears. A place to be healed.

A TV sits ten feet away. It is on, no one is watching.

They sit in silence, pressed and powdered.

Often they communicate in grunts and chin thrusts, but today, somehow, the rhythm is stopped. It is broken by my baba's voice.

How can we recreate this aberration.

It must start with his voice.

A rumble begins.

He turns to her, my grandmother. She is small, like me, but fair, a touch of Russian that my brown skin smothered, happily. Her legs are crossed, revealing slim ankles.

What is with her, he asks. Why was she wearing those shoes? She is acting strange. She has been acting strange.

I imagine a silence, in this quiet, empty house. But it is never quite here.

In the kitchen, far from this room a radio crackles out the new, 670am, Radio Iran.

In the backyard a gardener lets off a leaf blower and it roars echoing through the glass veranda.

She was looking forward while he spoke. Her eyes just left of the TV. Her glasses thick and tinted. She turns to him now. Not fully. One eye on him, one moving to the screen.

She is not a rough woman. Not my grandmother. My baba's wife she is someone else. My mother's mother, she is someone else. There was always a child in her. Maybe that is how our friendship started.

I am my grandmother's darling. The eldest granddaughter. We were allies and plotters once. She has always seen me. Never looking at the widening of hips in disgust, her directions, recommendations, loving observations never pierced me.

The phrase that comes out of her mouth cannot be told to you. It will be translated, directly, perfectly but only from her mouth, in her tongue could it be understood.

Through a roar and a crackle she says it to him, *what is it to you?*

What is it to you?

How this takes him aback

She is my lion.

He turns to her more fully now. A moment in shock where he must really see her. This woman who loves me dearly. He loves me dearly too.

I don't know this because he has said it, he has, here and there. I know this when I kiss him hello on

238

Fridays. When he picked me up from school and deposited me safely in my grandmother's arms.

My memories of him linger in hellos and goodbyes, in long hot drives, a car heavy with the smell of cigarettes and new leather.

Once, when I was young, awkward, and unathletic, my mom gave me a soccer ball, asked me to play with him. I needed to learn, but more importantly, I needed to let him teach me. We played on the lawn, or rather we stood across from each other and passed the ball back and forth.

I remember a Shabbat dinner, he and my brother face to face, he explaining that violence isn't the answer. My grandfather the soldier, telling my brother a young man, a young man, man to man, that fists solve nothing.

I remember my mother, sewing tags into new shirts, changing larges to mediums, he would only accept gifts in size medium.

I remember finding his knife and medals in the billiards room, wrapped in a soft uniform.

In his aging years he has begun his final lectures. It is a loop that will continue to the end.

Each child and grandchild a different track. Mine holds the line, you are going down the wrong path. Down the wrong path darling. Your friends are not your friends. One day you will wake with regrets. Many regrets.

I don't know this man well. My mother's father. But I have a feeling, that comes from deep in me, we are the same man. Except, I have my father's gentle, thoughtful eyes. My grandfather never liked those eyes.

He is not a poet. My grandfather. He is known to me by actions. By the children he has, my mother, and the house he has built for us.

I was raised in this house he built. I may not have slept there every night but in my imaginings of home, this is where I rest. He most strongly calls me back to the person I should have been.

He doesn't need me to agree on concepts of gender and politics, just on the needs of family. Of providing for those who have provided for you.

In the end who buries you.

This is not the job of a boy or a girl.

It is the job of a grandchild.

-S Kamran

Sounding it Out

Every December I get a card from my aunt in Puerto Rico. Every year, I open it and look for familiar Spanish words looping on the card. I recognize birthday, love, blessings. Bendeciones. It feels like how it feels when I go to say goodnight to my father. God bless you, he says, hugging me.

Sometimes she sends me cash wrapped in a napkin folded in the card. Sometimes she sends me a check (also folded in a napkin.) I pocket it and bring the card to my dad to read—first in warm Spanish, smoothly and softly. Then he tells me in English what she said, going for bigger meanings. She wishes me a happy birthday, hopes I'm well, asks for a picture, wants me to go to Puerto Rico one day. She tells me I'm beautiful. She's my father's sister and I am my father's daughter.

Every year, she writes on the card: Edsuvany Maisonet.

There's a script. Whether it's at the post office, the first day of class, or an interview. It's an icebreaker for me in Two Truths and a Lie. I have three middle names. My name is an amalgamation of my family members' names. I was named in an IHOP. Yes, thank

241

you, I know it's a beautiful/interesting/unique name. Make the smile reach my eyes for their sake, remember they'll be gone soon. Yes, it's a nickname. Move the conversation away. It's public but so personal. It's exhausting to crack myself open every time I meet someone. I haven't figured everything out and then I worry about how they're seeing my body, what they make of my voice and my clothes. I can't do it. I need the reminder sometimes that I don't have to. I am Edsuvani, the youngest of three daughters. I am Eddie, a lover, a brother, a friend, and fam's hijo. Most of the time, my name is Eddie. For others, my given name doesn't have much familiarity to hold on to. Thus in school I started to learn that about half way down the roster, it was easier to jump in at the confused hesitation. Sometimes I waited to see if they would try. Usually they stumbled over it. Often enough, stumbling over my name wasn't worth the trouble but she made the attempt.

"Eh... ed... suvini?"

"Edsuvani..."

The class tittered. Some of them turned towards the table to laugh. My face was warm. Eighth grade meant that this was ten years of this shit. It wasn't a surprise anymore still the laughter stung.

"... But you can call me Eddie."

It sat strangely in my stomach.

I think of all the words I use to articulate my body and experience and note how they feel inside me. Some of them make me feel knotted and hot, or tight in the way that travels up to my throat, or comfortable, peaceful even. I choose my names because if I don't there are a thousand other to mark my body. Naming myself is an attempt to navigate the violations—if I can't have my consent from them maybe I can try to claim my own autonomy. I find healing in the control, some reclamation in the respect communicated when someone uses the words I want. Most of the time, the words aren't right but they're more right than others.

I'm an Afro-Puerto Rican boi. I'm pretty and handsome. I'm loving, tender and gentle. I exist in unstable binaries. I am destructive and powerful. I'm a boi who wants to own his masculinity in all his beauty and violence and trauma. I'm a boi with a story and with a family history and generations of love culminating inside me. I'm a writer who's grasping for words to talk about this. I'm a writer who will ultimately fail but, goodness, is there grace in my failure because I'm trying still. I was definitely ashamed of my name when I was ashamed of my parents, my body, my family's apartment, my sister's pregnancy, anything. The shame meekly let others shorten and butcher my name. My mother was never ashamed of the name she gave me and once at the doctor's office, a nurse doing intake butchered my name. In the same tone my mother used when I got grease stains on my homework, she corrected the nurse. She would be out of the room and out of our lives in a few minutes and I didn't understand at the time why she was so aggressive, but I learned from my mom how to get angry.

At a summer job, my coworkers continued to call me "she" and somehow they kept forgetting. Anger terrifies me but I was angry. I felt the same bristling I heard in my mother's voice when our neighbors with familiar, brown skin fawned over her hijito, ayy que lindo, ello. I've always looked like a little boy—a pretty one—but still. However, there was that shift from when my mother could laugh off my tomboyish preference for boys' husky jeans and Pokemon tee shirts to mildly annoyed when it stopped being cute. Mild annoyance became a problem.

Soon, that tone was there when she asked me if my boy friends were my boyfriends. (In hindsight, she might have been simultaneously hopeful.) She wanted to know why I didn't play with the girls. (In hindsight, I'm not quite sure if she truly would have liked that more.) Her middle school age tomboy daughter didn't start begging to dress in the juniors' section and could feel her embarrassment when she was "he'd." Still, at the root maybe our anger is really the same.

The shame isn't the same as it was. I have no problem claiming my given name, for it's my bond to my family and our tumultuous relationship. It's not a "birth name", which reflects a severing from the past. Sometimes I say full name, but Eddie sounds as full between my love's lips as Edsuvani. Finding truth in naming means navigating failures of language. I met a young transgender man who was doing a photo project capturing portraits of queer youth. (I was the only brown person.) Bluntly put, he was a lesson when I met him—a culmination of all the critiques of young queers finding masculinity and the violences they can commit. Over time we grew into a uniquely intimate friendship.

One day, I went over to shoot in his studio. He and his mother picked me up from the suburban train station. There was small talk for a few minutes and, all of a sudden, his mother asked me in a conversation about my work in the Afro-American Studies department if I knew my history and it shook me. In his house, he asked me when I was going to change my name and all the words I had practiced fell away from me. I wanted to yell and be articulately angry—I am proud of my name is and that's not something I need to do, not everyone is transitioning to be a white man— but I could only stammer out, feeling young and confused and all soft lines, "I don't think I'm going to do that." It's a bold question, if I had ever doubted the fact that there was an intimacy between us, I knew then he felt it. She calls me by my given name sometimes. I let them call me by my given name, sometimes. Sometimes, she chooses to call me by my given name when we're close and our voices are quiet.

Their name is beautiful, but it's torn too. One of the first times we spoke over Skype, we talked about our names. I was afraid to mess it up and her name in my phone was their nickname. When we hung up, I went over the letters in my head, trying my hardest to fit them together. I needed to get it right. I told her my given name. It was urgent. We are both daughters with difficult names, loaded names. Heavy names. Beautiful names. We are bois figuring out how to wear those names, our histories. The names afford us some security in meeting people. You can tell a lot about someone from how the handle your name. Do they stumble through it? Do they fuck up and try again?

Does the apology in their words reach their eyes? Do they ask you to say it, take it in and try to follow the motions of your lips? They call me by my given name sometimes. I let her call me by my given name, sometimes. Sometimes, they choose to call me by my given name when we're close and our voices are quiet.

Home is always a hard place but this name is where I find it. It's where I'm trying to build home out of words and bandages. I decide who to let in and when I do, I expect them to handle these words tenderly. I've cracked myself open to this person and they became a part of my story that begins at the IHOP where my family put me together from them parts of each of their names. On a page, I have to reconcile the nicknames at home and the foreignness of professors using my whole name, and being a "he" some places and struggling with how I relate to my family. Who I am fucks with linear time and makes words hard to pin down but it's all I've got.

But still, maybe there needn't be formal reconciliation because regardless, here I am.

-Eddie Maisonet

Raising Another Man's Baby

Two days ago while engaged in some very serious Barbie play, my daughter told me that even though I'm her Mommy J, I'm still the daddy..." Taken aback" is an understatement.

It's crazy to think that not too long ago I was a young AG in the village, du-rag and fitted clad picking up femmes with corny pickup lines and talking shit with my bois. On a nightly basis, a street corner quartet of machismo played out in front of Papaya Dog and the neon buzz of ubiquitous sex-toyshops. It was only a matter of time amidst the big booties, fierce queens, and ladies of the night, that a straight couple would come walking by. More often than not, the male in the pairing would grab onto his girl as a display of hyper masculine ownership to ward off advances from the bois on the corner. Perhaps it was the sheer debauchery of a mannequin dressed in a nun costume, wearing chaps and a ball gag in its mouth in the window behind us, either way, the dude would always shield his woman from the village pariahs.

These exchanges would always spark the same

questions around the role men play in our community and relationships. Bi, curious, bi-curious, fluid or just "free spirited" women were and still are a reality within the lesbian scene and opinions of this reality have never been scarce on either side of the coin.

Like clockwork, the same barrage of questions ensued:

Would you be cool if your girl messed with a dude while messing with you

Fuck outta here. If you're with me you're with me...Unless she wants to bring another femme in the mix.

Does it mean more when you break up with a girl and she goes back to dating dudes?

Hell yea. She just wants that nigga cause he has a dick.

Do you date straight girls?

Bruh, you know I turn them out on the reg.

Would you date a girl with kids?

I don't know, man. I'm not beat for no badass kids and I'll never raise another man's baby.

* * *

My bravado would never have me play second fiddle to a non-existent father who was fortuitous enough to have a penis. While I would never call it jealousy that a man could get a woman pregnant, there is something desirable about not having to jump through laborious and rather expensive hoops to have a child; I wouldn't mind going half on a baby with the woman I love. Aside from the influence of gender roles and complexities of being a young masculine-identified female, the realities of having children and being a lesbian were already on my mind.

Tongue in cheek at first, I thought I would never be faced with the question. Having been in a very long-term relationship, I was certain I didn't have anything to worry about. After I completed grad school, my partner of nine years and I would start to plan out having a family through in-vitro, surrogacy, or sibling assisted fertilization. During one of our "breaks" the question became all too real when she told me she was pregnant. In true lesbian form, we were still living together and dating other people, taking time (not space) apart from each other to work on our friendship and be better for one another.

In an instant, that friendship and relationship was destroyed beyond repair and I was faced with the unlikely scenario of an unplanned pregnancy in a lesbian relationship.

The Decision to stay was not an easy one. After the initial shock and whiskey-soaked tears, my ex at the time was rather understanding. She was keeping the baby and had zero expectations of me and the non-existent baby's father. This was her responsibility and she would do what she had to do as a mother. You may ask: what decision, then, did I have to make? She wasn't my girl anymore, and clearly it wasn't my baby. She had no expectations of me, so I should've just sent her packing and moved on, right?

There was a side of me that wanted nothing more than to do that. Not only was I disappointed, but the resentment I felt was palpable: she took my future family away. This was vastly different than some random ex of yours having a child. We were still engaging with one another and living together, while not "together-together." From the moment she told me, the reality that we could no longer go through the exciting yet nerve-racking process of planning *our* first child sunk in. I had no say in the timing of conception, my family couldn't share their input regarding the process and the weight of all of this hit me like a ton of bricks. Everyday, I woke up in a cloud of anger, resentment and with hangover headache. I would drink until I didn't feel the sting of the pain and living with her was bearable.

It wasn't until my baby mama had a real-deal conversation with me that I stopped wallowing, and started acting like an adult. Once I made the decision to be involved, she made it a point to make sure I wasn't staying because I pitied her, or in hopes that this would save us—but, that I was deciding to be involved for the child. With a simple gesture of buying a baby book and placing it on my baby mama's pillow, I was all in for my baby girl.

I'm not going to lie, it's no surprise why some people have children to fix a failing relationship. The excitement and anticipation of a new baby has a remarkable ability to make you forget about the resentment, pain, and the initial relationship problems that lead to the breakup and subsequent conception in the first place. Watching her belly grow and learning about the baby's development was pretty cool. The best part was feeling my unborn child respond to me while in the womb, getting excited when she would hear my voice, or dance around in my baby mama's belly when I played my country music. It became all too apparent that a real person was forming in there, and I was nothing short of ecstatic to be along for the ride.

The Struggle of staying began to subside as time went on. Not too many things in this world make you forget about the drama of adult life than the expectation of a new one. As I threw myself into the excitement of my daughter's arrival, the resentment and pain associated with her conception diminished and the joy of creating a family unit emerged. Once my daughter was born, in the most ironic of plot twists, she came out looking just like me. Friends, family, co-workers, doctors, nurses and folks on social media were and continue to be astonished by how much my daughter is my 'mini-me.' According to folklore, an expecting mother's child comes out looking like the person who annoyed them the most while they were pregnant. Either way, I'll take it.

A really random and unforeseen struggle as a result of my decision to parent is the misconception that I and my baby mama used my daughter's biological father to create a kid of our own. I cringe as I write this, and remain surprised it withstood all of my edits because it is nothing short of absurd. Never in a million years would I wish that experience on anyone. And frankly, if I had my choice in the matter, I'm not too sure I would've picked him; but my daughter is perfect, so I can't say that with 100% certainty. Thank God for the fluidity within the nurture vs. nature paradigm.

I digress. We rode that wave of excitement for a while until the tide came in and washed up all of the issues we had forgotten about. Neither of us remembers the turning point, but we started to lose track of the love we had for each other and focused solely on our daughter. By the time we looked up, we realized we were staying in a relationship for her sake, and not because we were in love with each other. Resentment gave way to mistrust, apathy and "acting out" to the point where being together was toxic. Our daughter was approaching the age where she was able to interpret what's going on around her, and we refused to be a bad example for her. We decided to break up and six months later, my baby mama and daughter moved out.

Naturally a new struggle arose; co-parenting from a distance. There was no question, my commitment to my daughter was and is the same whether I am with her mother or not. My baby mama respected that, and honestly didn't expect anything less from me. In the face of dating other folks, navigating a breakup and trying to salvage a friendship, we continue to make it past the growing pains and into a space that is completely focused on our daughter and an example of a healthy parental relationship. The road to this space has been laden with countless setbacks but some triumphs too.

Over time the struggle was no longer around my willingness to parent, but how that willingness affects the people around me—namely any current or future love interests. Having been a lover and overall admirer of women for more than two decades, I have come to understand that telling the woman you're dating that you are in constant communication with your ex (and baby mama) doesn't go over very well. It's hard for a non-parent to understand that you will do whatever it takes for your child, even staying in contact with your ex when a new girlfriend may not like it. What if the woman of my dreams doesn't want kids off the bat?

What if she is the jealous type and having an ex in your life is a non- negotiable? I'm thankful that at this point that I have found a woman who loves me, and most importantly, loves me for being committed to my child. Does that mean it's easy all the time? No, but she would never do anything to jeopardize or impede my relationship with my daughter and does, in fact, understand why I talk to my baby mama on a regular basis.

The Future is nothing short of bittersweet. My daughter is literally the most awesome human being on this earth (besides her mother—not the other one), but like any parent I fear that my decisions will impact my child negatively. Elementary school has become a preverbal war zone where kids are scrutinized for every aspect of who they are, what they look like, and often times, who their parents are. Will I become a soft spot for bullies? Will she understand who I am to her being that I'm not with her mother? Will she even want me around when her mother gets married and I am not a part of the familial unit?

One continuous struggle, is the societal imposition of gender roles and socially acceptable family paradigms on my daughter. While my daughter was in daycare, we would continually have to tell her teachers that her Valentine's Day artwork shouldn't say "I love you Mom and Dad," or that at the age of three, there's no way she can understand that out of two mommies, one doesn't have to be a daddy. To the credit of my baby mama and myself, we are raising a rather well-adjusted, intelligent, beautiful little girl who knows she can be whatever she wants to be when she grows up. She even asks why all the skateboards in

Target are blue and not pink because she wants to ride one like her Mommy J (that's my girl!).

I pray that the future also holds healing for myself, but most importantly, my baby mother. The one thing I underestimated was the toll resentment takes on a person. I didn't recognize the ways it manifested itself in both, small and rather, large ways. To say that I began to hate my ex after she told me she was pregnant is a little too aggressive. The unresolved, and frankly, unacknowledged resentment I felt made me fall out of love with her. To this day it is hard to fully articulate, but I never got over the fact that she got pregnant. No matter how excited I was about the new baby, I still harbored negative emotions towards my baby mama.

I really wanted "love to conquer all," for this child to make us happy again, and force us back into love, but it doesn't work that way. It's unfair to put those expectations on a child, but I did. Even now, years later, it is difficult for me to admit it: I was weak, immature and unable to handle the tough situation placed in front of me. With time and tough conversations I am sure that the wounds will heal and we will be a productive, yet modern familial unit.

My life is a romantic-comedy-thriller, in which the plot takes sudden turns and what you see isn't always what it appears to be. My daughter's father, who at one point was hundreds of miles away, now is back with my baby mother romantically. From the very beginning, I was a proponent for him to be in her life, we all know a young lady with daddy issues can be faced with a whole host of difficulties, none of which I want for my little girl (I'm not a champion of the belief that a child *needs* their father; I do believe a child *needs* love). In terms of being with my baby mother, I'm all for whatever makes her happy and is best for my daughter. That being said, his presence has opened up some new struggles that I did not anticipate. Where do I, as a non-bio mother, fit into the picture when both of my daughter's parents are in the household? Is there space for me? Should I even be in the mix as a parent? Why do I feel displaced when he was absent from his child's life?

I grapple with the validity of all of my fears, to this day, at the age of three (going on four in two months) my daughter has my wit and sarcasm, excellent taste in music, and is brilliant. I have a baby mama who is understanding and supportive of the relationship I have with my daughter. My family loves my daughter and accepts her as their own. My child is being raised with nothing but love and good people around her. So, I couldn't ask for anything more. I often joke about my daughter's almost certain future of two mommies, one daddy, and a stepmom at parent-teacher conferences, I know she wouldn't be amused, but sounds rather entertaining.

I continue to make sure my daughter knows no matter what, I'm not going anywhere. My commitment to her is something I've made independent of the intimacy and relationship I have with her mother. At this point, the mother of my child, who is farthest from the stigmatized popular 'Baby Mama' trope, has nothing but respect for the parental relationship I have with my daughter, which I can admit is rare.

The Silence is overwhelming. A larger narrative and recent interest of mine is the strengthening of ties between the Gen X, millennial, and Gen Y masculine-identified lesbians and the OG AGs, from the '60s and later. The access to the experience and knowledge held by the folks who have lived this life through social and institutional peril and who have done the work that makes us bois shooting-the-shit on the corner possible is invaluable and necessary. As alluded to earlier, I don't have other masculine identified lesbians who have been through similar situations to talk to or gain wisdom from. I understand that no one has all of the answers, but support and experience can help volumes.

Outside of the generational divide, there is a bit of a taboo around the topic of raising children who aren't biologically "yours." By no means is this estimation scientific, but most of the masculine-identified lesbians I know have been in a relationship with a woman who has had children or who were pregnant. Out of the four bois that comprise my inner circle, all of us have played a parental role to our girlfriends' kids, and have subsequently had to navigate the relationship between the mother, and the relationship with the child after a breakup. More often than not, ties with the child are broken once the relationship with the mother ends. In addition, positive co-parenting fails in the face of 'Baby Mama Drama' or wishy-washy, non-bio mom involvement.

I've gotten some pushback from members in our community for my choice to be a mother instead of a father or pseudo-father figure. Perhaps it is my age or what I've been through that makes me steadfast in my choice. My choice of clothing does not dictate my parental role. I embrace being a woman and enjoy teaching my daughter that 'woman' includes riding pink skateboards and wearing khaki's with boat shoes if she so chooses. By the very nature of those who identify as female or woman, we are predetermined to nurture the children and people who are related to us, as well as those who are not. I am proud to be a mother with struggles, flaws, non-ideal situation and all. Personally, I have not lived this life as a man, and while I can extrapolate and read accounts, I do not have that perspective, and don't pretend to. Once my daughter reaches a certain age, that'll become rather confusing, rather quickly. Regardless of the title that my child calls me, she will receive the same love, and same developmental lessons.

This piece was important to me not only for its cathartic benefits, but to get the conversation going. What does it mean to be a parent as a masculine-identified lesbian? What are the stories and lessons we can share with each other regarding navigating this tough but rewarding terrain? I am not unrealistic and through the process of writing this piece I am reminded as to why this is hard to share. It is ok for bois to feel and cry, and share that they've been tough times. That they've loved and lost, and perhaps at times were not able to measure up to their own expectations. Through the opening of this dialogue I hope we, as a community, are inspired to commune around our shared experiences, both negative and positive. My anecdote above is literally just the beginning. My story is laden with many more twists, turns, mistakes, and some triumphs—all of which are valuable lessons to share so we no longer feel as if we suffer alone.

-J. Handy

Two Spirit and Gender Spirituality

I was supposed to have long hair. That was one of the promises my mother made to my grandmother when it became clear that we were emigrating to the United States. Long hair, a sign of virginity, belief in God and obedience. I was supposed to have long hair and It would be considered a sign of disloyalty and needless rebellion to trim its lengths. By the time I was nine years old, it was down to my knees. The wavy strands would curl onto my back in my sleep and after showers would be pulled into a tower above me with a comb and strong arms. I felt like a sculpture, a rebellious one at that. I disobeyed and one day I braided gum into the curls of my long braid. In tears my mother closed the mouth of long arm scissors and broke fibers of my hair while I broke familial expectations. As with gender, I have broken colonized expectations while keeping faith in the survival of my people. I choose to believe that gender is part of my spirituality, that I never lost my way.

Being born with the inherited shame of being Indigenous in an Indigenous hating-country, I also inherited the pain and loss of broken connections. What I know now is that because of colonization, I was, my grandmother was, and we are born into a white Eurocentric gender binary. For this reason I believe gender binary is a form of settler colonialism and deeply connected to white supremacy. My family took to the church to redeem their social value, and in the process continued to pass down a spirituality that is deeply shaped by the strong arms of Indigeneity. Due to inconsistent record keeping as a result of illiteracy and lack of education in my family, I can't trace back the last generation that lived without fear of expressing gender differently than that of the Spanish colonizers. Being born into white gender complicates how I relate to words meant to describe genders outside of the binary. I identify as a female assigned at birth two spirit person although I use the words genderqueer and transgender to explain myself to new people in my life. I know that these terms too are a result of colonization. If the gender binary is the norm, and we must create words to distinguish ourselves apart from the binary, do we ever move away from white Eurocentric gender? I often think about that.

The truth is that I don't know what it was like for my Purepecha ancestors before the Friars came to convert them to Catholicism and Eurocentric standards of being. Colonization was a force that moved my ancestors from villages to mountains. In modern times this tradition of hiding has continued by negating Indigenous ancestry in order to try to appear more Spanish and therefore more worth surviving in clear sight. We survive/d by hiding. And this way of surviving is still something that I feel deeply in my body. At times genderqueer feels like a veil over me, a word meant to cover up this sacred part of me that people assume is simple. Much like the misunderstanding and oversimplification of Indigenous identities, I feel that words like genderqueer and transgender oversimplify gender.

Oversimplification serves the privileged by making othered people work around the systems that disenfranchise them. My question to those coming out of hiding, people like myself who have gone through the process of revealing ancestral connection, is how do we reconcile gender using today's language while acknowledging our history? How do you live a gender that is authentic to us without romanticizing our ancestor's experience of gender? I ask this because the act of inviting the invisible to become visible is painful. I also ask this because of how harmful romanticization of Indigenous roots is to the Indigenous people who are alive today; to treat Indigenous people as if they are dead entities, only valuable of grave robbed references for depth. I often tell people that revealing my Indigeneity has been more painful than expressing my gender. This is true for me because of how deeply intertwined gender is to colonization, and how much colonization has severed my connection to my Indigenous roots.

My gender is part of my spirituality because there is so much left that is unknown and spirituality means believing in things without proof. I believe that my gender, my binary crossing is something that my ancestors would be proud of. Beyond words, I believe that there can be spirituality in living an authentic, ever changing gender. This process of reconciling my gender in a way that honors and does not romanticize my ancestors is one acknowledging the unknown. It is one of admitting that there are things that research will not reveal about how gender was expressed before colonization. As an Indigenous person raised without my culture, within Mestizo communities, I learned what it was to be Purepecha in the negative comments said to any person who dared to defy the norms. This way of acknowledging the unknown is the same practice I use towards my gender. I know that time will reveal more about how I relate to masculinity and femininity. I know that I am not fixed, that gender is sacred. It cannot be explained in simple words or in opposition to the gender binary we live in. It is intimacy. Since I have little to go on about gender before colonization, I turn to intimacy as my moment of reclamation. Revealing my true gender is a unveiling and peeling back of words that cannot touch the sacrament of how complex my gender is. I know I am not alone in this.

-Fabian Romero

Contractions

We left the retreat center, as assigned, in silence, breathing. Taking in the small Mississippi town, the houses and the manicured yards, the narrow country roads, and as suggested by our sister-doctor-facilitator, I wondered if I should try to hold Monica's hand. We were there in remembrance of Ella Baker, Fannie Lou Hamer, Amzie and Ruth Moore, SNCC and Freedom Summer. We passed a set of tall magnolias bordering the street, meditating on the sky, their moss-covered roots holding each other, making a web-like frame around the ground between them.

I offered my palm to Monica, who smiled, pressed her east coast southern into my open desert. Meditating on contours of a Black woman's hand felt like the most radical thing I'd ever done. We walked in the middle of the street. And I stared down the drivers who had to move for us.

Two months earlier in Tempe, campus police wrestled a Black woman professor to the ground for not showing ID. Charged her with felony assault of an officer. Two months later the police stopped a Black teen for not being on the sidewalk. Shot him dead. For picking up an air rifle in a Walmart Choked another for selling cigarettes. Ms. Deloris, the owner of the retreat center, told us that we were in what used to be high klan country. Monica closed her eyes. When we passed in front of the police station and courthouse my whole body clenched, hardened to all the dead Black bodies between us and them. We walked, breathing, Magnolia. Our clasped palms kissing as our bodies pressed redemption through the asphalt under our feet.

* * *

Grandma Mary Cruz (Moore) Owens stared at my neck. What is that. A mole?

You should see a doctor. Have it removed.

I can take it off myself, I tell her. With thread. I've done it before. It's 11:00 p.m., and she's just brought me home from the airport.

She stands by the stove finishing the manchupa for the ladies at the bank.

Will you tell me about my name? At a recent training making a name tag woke up a shiftiness that seemed to sleep so close to my surface lately. I wrote Maria in big letters. Then squeezed Matice underneath, introduced myself to the group as both.

She says in her thick, Cape Verdian accent. Maria DaLuz. You were named for your great great grandmother,

I felt my first name in my mouth. Noticed the kitchen to look closely at my neck. Reaches in the pantry.

Here's some thread. Gives me the spool and returns to her stew,how the r plateaued, unrolled by my family's proximity to Boston. It was really hot, and

263

you were slow. The last time the doctors sent your parents home to wait they just stayed in the hospital parking lot. determined to stay with the middle. Your Dad was so moved afterward he changed your name to Maria Matice. Grandma crosses ignoring the scraggly hairs of my goatee.

After two weeks, I drew a line through my first name unsteady, but I can't imagine what it's like Transitioning between names is full of starts and stops. The new (old) name feels to wear a name so finely tailored it covers everything.

When it was my turn to reciprocate with naked pictures it took me well over an hour to reconcile with being shot. They said, some people are into large breasted bois. I said, I'm into seeing myself from the mid-chest up so I can imagine what I might be like after surgery. Looked at my whole curvy body, remembered my mother naked in front of the dresser, a thick waxy brown line down the inner side of her full, oblong breast. They were benign, she said, showing me the other, the two scars facing like parallel lines. Fibroid tumors they didn't have to take. I decided to wear my strap under pants unzipped at the waist. 20 years later my Mom was so angry when the doctors insisted on the double mastectomy. She refused.

Snap. I held a heaping handful of heavy tissue firmly to my chest and framed the nipple between my fingers.

Snap. Imagined how much I loved letting long breasts flow over eager lips and into wet hungry mouths. Between blood and air potential pulsing.

Once on an overnight shift next to my mother's armchair, I listened to the breathing machine push. She strained for air in short constant gasps too weak now to cough up the phlegm filled fluid that was crushing her lungs. Supposedly the body can make cancer cells for decades before they clump and are detected. I waited on her drowning in an armchair. Hungry mutant cells determined to multiply. To shove their way into being and make waste fluid. Breathe. Mom.Breathe. Mattie (Lucille) Lavender-Moore.

Grieve all of them.

Once we were transitioning in a hot car in Phoenix, both of us pushing from one they to another. Waiting to know his future breasts to nurture, her bones to ashes.

-Matice Moore

Stageplay

ACT I
Scene 1

BILLIE

The first group meeting in the girl's wing of the Alameda County Juvenile Detention Center is always the same. Introductions first, then stories about why we are here, all exaggerated. Then some sort of test to see who will break, I got ten dollars on you.

Truth is, I can call every story in here, it's my fifth time, they start to repeat themselves after the third. (Points to audience)

You ran a little bag of weed for your boy and got caught, you jacked some of those expensive bras from that lingerie shop on Broadway, and you're the girl who punched one of your teachers in the face when she called you stupid? Damn. I guess it's my turn.

My name is Billie, like the one who sings the blues. If it was up to my mother they would still call me Marcy, a mark of a name given by that mark my mother married, Marcus.

Marcus makes moments for money, moves motion to mold movies, I asked him to put me in one, he asked my mother to put me out.

Psh. it's a bitch being homeless on house arrest.

Most think moms threw me out because of Marcus. Nope. Moms threw me out because of these here black jeans, I haven't taken them off for days, can't say I took her by surprise. She was just so sure she didn't raise that type of black girl you know? Half blue and all boy.

So I bought these here real boy jeans from this real boy in my class. 34 waist, big enough to sag over my hoop shorts and shit. Everyone knew that every real boy hooped during lunch. Rule #3 in the real boy rule book. Been clocking real boys for real long, since like eighth grade. Three whole years, I know the rules like nothing else.

So Alden sold me these here jeans for $10, a red Gatorade, and two blank passes to excuse him from class at any time; I'd tell you where I copped the passes but that's against real boy rule #6. Never start snitching.

So right when I got these here jeans, I walked all the way to the other side of campus, to the handicap bathrooms. You know those stupid blue signs that be on the outside of them? The ones with the stupid stick chick in the triangle dress. This one didn't have none of that, first time I noticed.

Soon as I got into that stall I took off my fake girl jeans, they were the closest thing to real boy jeans moms would let me get. You know, straight legged but making too much of a woman out of my waist.

Once I had them off I pulled my favorite pair of boxers from my hoop bag, they were plaid and shit. I bought them last year at the Abercrombie Outlet in Pismo while on family vacay with my first crush. My first time joints. I slid them on… my fake girl jeans wouldn't fit over them before so this was new. Before I jumped into real boyhood, I held up my real boy jeans to the door.

I was ready.

I walked out of that bathroom juiced. Looked at that mirror, stuck. I was smiling but stuck. That mirror, that same ass mirror that used to show me as that guilty ass girl, showed me some boy. Some black boy. Some real cute black boy. Yo, but real boy rule #16 never let them know that you know you're cute.

I had on this double XL white T that was way too big, but it looked tight, precise. I was also wearing my J's that day, only pair, the same pair I had to have a family meeting about. It had to be voted whether or not I was responsible enough to own them.

I guess my parents thought I was, as long as I was responsible enough to pay for them myself. Four weeks of work. So I shined them that day, seemed appropriate. My hair was not shinny that day, or any other day, but I ran my fingers through it anyway. This shit is nappy right? Dry and thick. All the things mothers hope their first black born's hair isn't. But I loved that boy. That cute boy. That real cute black boy.

I was shook my first few steps, it always happened this way. This time instead of being worried that someone was gonna see me in my fake girl jeans and think I was cute, I was just hella worried about some chick seeing me as this real boy and think I was gross.

Damn, My nerves were high, like I should've been, but I skipped blunts with Bini at the creek that morning to stay focused, real focused.

So I was focused right, on the walk. On getting my smooth on, on feeling the power while I paced. I walked to the middle hallways, middle runway for my debut. I looked at the watch my grandmother gave me the same day she called me handsome. It was time.

I walked down that hallway waiting to be ridiculed. Worried about what I was wearing, was it wavy? It was, so I walked and it went perfectly. I got the usual nods from the Nortes and the stern shakes from the squares. No one even noticed. Not even Ms. Navarro, who came up to me earlier that day.

MS. NAVARRO
Billie, sit up straight. Chest out. Cross your legs. Act more like a lady Billie. Smile. Stop being so blue, so boy, it's not very becoming.

BILLIE
As soon as I reached the end of the hall, I turned to my locker. I was free and could breath. I pulled up my pants like all boys do, all real boys. With both arms behind them at 90 degrees, knees slightly bent. Real boy rule #33. It's the stance you learn when you first learn to fight, one foot a little in front of the other, it gives you power. Lets your opponent know " I'm ready for you muthafucka." I was ready for any muthafucka to come near me and say something smart, they'd catch a real quick one to the face. Bet. Just as I was getting ready to get out, some one came to take me up on my offer, I turned around and it was moms.

Now normally moms doesn't just come showing up at school. That act alone is a major violation, breaks three real boy rules at the same time. Rule #38,

Rule #21 and Rule #3. Which all state in slight variations that one's turf shall never be infiltrated, especially by moms. But there she was. Mean and mugging as ever, and it had to be today. The day I fell in love with a real boy.

(Billie takes her hat off and turns into moms)

MOMS
Look at my Marcy all manned up. Ha, good thing your P.O. called and said you'd been missing meetings. He wanted to make sure you were making it to class and I haven't seen my baby girl in a few days, has it been a week? I wanted to check on you, and look what I come to find.

BILLIE
I didn't fight cuz I've seen Moms bare knuckle box in the backyard with real boys before. She walked me back down the hallway, smirking like she smelled something sweet. As we left the front gate security asked why I was leaving. Moms said I was sick.

I was forced into our family Ford. The same truck I used to sneak out to see Tracy. I was stealthy then, under the radar. Barley blasphemous before these britches for real boys.

We sat in silence for a while and Moms started to drive home. For six miles we seldom spoke, she smoked, I sat staring.

Billie trades places in the car and becomes Moms.

MOMS
Downtown hospital room 222, my little brown baby was born. I wish you could remember Marcy, I was so

proud to be your mother. You never think so much of yourself until you're somebody's whole world you know? I wish you loved me like I loved you. Like you loved running. I used to run when I was young too, and a bit when I was older, and those few times when you were little and once when you got bigger. The way home gets fuzzy after a while, you know that. You always seem to make your way back.

(beat)

Why are your jeans black? Where are the blue ones I bought you? The ones with the waist? Why won't you wear them? Why won't you walk like a woman? You wanna be a man, Marcy? Play GOD for a little while? Make a big mess of what the big man made you.

You think you bold? It's like you think those breasts are for boys. You know they'll call you queer right? and Dyke, and butch bitch. You won't have a white dress or a wedding Marcy. How are you going to have kids? Ugh, how could you love another girl? You're supposed to fall in love with a real boy.

You're not slick either, thought I wouldn't notice how you've been changing? It's been years, living in your hoop shorts, you don't care about you. You don't care how you look, writing little lesbian love notes.

You should see the way people look at me when I tell them that you're my daughter. I've tried, GOD, I've tried. I met you halfway, stopped asking you to wear shorts, not saying anything about those ripped shirts that are way too big. You used to care, used to humor me at least with those cute pink tops, had the decency to get dressed around me.

What did I do to you?

(Billie gets back in the other seat)

271

BILLIE

It was harsh, but it happens. Well has happened a heaping a handful of times, the first few I had my guard down. Was unprepared on purpose, hoping she'd take me back. I'm no fool though.

After the second time I started packing my day bag with things one might need on the everyday; a toothbrush, bowers, toothpaste, a pencil, socks, snacks when they would fit, a phone when it was paid for, and a bus pass if I found one. I always left my I.D. though, just in case I got picked up, the cops should have a hard time too shit. Trynna find out who I am. After Moms sped up and sped off, I spent the next two hours walking towards something safe. Today I didn't have much, no money, no motivation, no Moms to be mad when I came home near midnight, at least I have the boy I loved. After the tension and the tears, I tore open my gym bag and slid my real boy jeans back on. I kissed that black boy I loved and kept moving.

-Nappy Nina

Her Ex-Boifriend

I send her flowers just because...

So on the day when I must lay them on her grave,
it won't be a farewell gesture
but a manifestation of my love.

I give her Roses on Sunday's,
Lilly's on Tuesdays,
Orchids on Wednesday,
and sunflowers every other Friday...

Because he never did.

So she plucked love notes to float
in puddles of her disappointed desires for his attention
to lovers affection.

He neglected the small things...
Like pink and white plastic sticks
crimson stained by hints of fetus
thrown in steel bins on prom night.

I send red roses for her two C-section births,
two miscarriages, and one hysterectomy,

in celebration of the blood she scarified for life to
flourish from her body.

White Calla Lily's idolize her
posture on Tuesdays
greener with envy than
the cellulose synthesis in their cytoplasm.

My pulse to the world.
Gatekeeper to reality.

My mother adores orchids,
these spring ornaments
adorn her mantles
in vases like beta fish in pet store windows
in the 2000's on black Friday before 8 a.m. Santa
Claus wish list shopping antics
turn to arrest and public humiliation.

I send her flowers because sometimes
her love feels like I'm one of her ex-boyfriends...
An on again off again relationship.
On for as long as I'm doing what she likes,
but so much of it is off again...
and I'll just be her trans son she can't quite understand,

who sends flowers hoping to win the love of my
mother and reconcile with her this lifetime.

I don't want to be her ex-boifriend anymore.

-Lex Kennedy

My Name Is Dirt

My Brother

During my formative years, I was raised by mud-soaked crawfish, at least part of the time. My brother, a mere year and a half younger, and I would join the swarm of neighborhood kids to find the fastest ways to destroy our white sneakers, and scrape our brown legs, in the thread-bare woods behind our suburban cul-de-sac.

Sometimes we didn't have to go very far to collect our favorite shelled creatures. They dwelled in the grassy sewer drain tunnels, under giant jagged rocks, along the lawn swells that sat next to the well-paved streets. We gripped the rock's edges with our small hands, pulled upward its weight with our tiny bodies, and uncovered the mysteries underneath the murky water.

We impatiently waited a moment—then two, then three—to learn our luck. Once the mud cloud cleared, we either saw more mud, scurrying legs, or beady eyes pointed toward us. My chest puffed with pride when I lifted the heaviest rock, three times the size of my dark bony arms, balanced its heft with my left hand, and snatched a bare palm-full of a crawfish with the other.

The thrill was in the surprise as the rock was

barely separated from its mildewed under-sludge. I enjoyed the chase through the shallow backwash. I always returned the terrified crustacean to its muddy place in the Earth; its indentation disappeared by runny dirt eager to re-form the surface. I never intended to displace it from its home—I was just always drawn to its life in the dirt, hidden away from artificial surroundings that had sprung all around it.

Crawfish hunts were one of my favorite outdoor pastimes with my brother. He and I looked too different to be confused with one another, his curly bunch of black curls contrasted against my short dark-haired pony tail, and the complexion on which our hair sat were shades apart—his a light milky caramel color, and mine a soil-rich, and yellow under-toned. Yet, we understood that we resembled twins to some neighbors who, upon seeing a brown blur pass by on foot, may have assumed that the pair of energetic children running by, compressed within boy's T-shirts and jeans, were in fact brothers. Years later I would understand that our kid-play was my natural way of being, not to be discarded as the stuff of childish invention.

My Father

It's true that my brother and I wore virtually matching clothes for my first 13 years of our lives, until middle school when my brother doubled in size overnight, and I transformed into a metal-punk geek by adopting parachute khakis, oversized band T-shirts, and metal jewelry.

The days dwindled when my father could proudly bestow us matching T-shirts when he returned from out-of-town conferences, and gladly stretch a boy's cotton shirt imprinted with a brightly colored city name across my shoulders, then my brother's. I instead requested shot glass gifts without a hint of sarcasm as adolescence descended. My earnest father, adoring of his two unique children, began to bring home a shot glass for his peculiar daughter and matching T-shirts from the far away cities that he visited. He lovingly continued to bring us gifts until I grew, until a young college-bound adult thought the T-shirts were replaced by random trinkets that he thought we'd like, and of course, a shot glass for his daughter's sizeable collection.

On a visit to my father's home, during my sophomore year of college, he treated my brother and me to dinner at one of those generic "nouveaux" chain restaurants that tend to be popular in rich suburbs. It was a forgettable place across the street from his gated community but a lavish outing that my father enjoyed paying for as yet another sign of his devotion to us. We, not so secretly, enjoyed the outings too, as evidenced by our $40 tabs.

My father occupied one side of the booth with a cadre of things resting next to him, and we squeezed into the other side as we always had. Soon, my father's face grew solemn as we rummaged through our plentiful appetizers and multiple frothy drinks. I sensed what was to come. His sentimental expression surfaced and he extended his hands across the table. My brother and I each awkwardly rested a hand into his large open-palms.

"I'm so proud of you both. Richael, my wonderful daughter, my angel from the airplane. And Bobby, my talented son, my little rock star!"

He stared at us for several long moments as wet beads formed wells along the rims of his eyes. Before the tears trickled over, he reached to a plastic gift bag next to him. Our eyes darted from the mystery bag to each other in anticipation for unknown souvenir that was inside. I squinted to behold what my father unveiled at the table—he clumsily lifted two SpongeBob Squarepants pairs of shorts over our ornate lemon-accented water glasses.

My brother and I turned toward each other in embarrassed sibling disbelief. Is our father really giving us SpongeBob shorts during dinner, at a public restaurant, where we were knew people?

We had known our father to be relatively shameless about conducting private conversations in very public places. He meant no harm; he was just unfortunately aloof about these things. But as we looked closer at the gifts dangling above our cold butter rolls, we suddenly realized that we were wrong—he was utterly immune to humiliation. Our limp hands received not only SpongeBob Squarepants shorts, but bejeweled boxer shorts. He was gifting us matching underwear, during dinner, at a public restaurant, where we knew people.

Once realization set in, we quickly snatched the boxers from across the table. In my hurried rush to remove the boxers from sight, my fingers caught on the giant slit across the middle of the shorts. It dropped on me like a ton of wet sponges: my father assumed that I wore men's boxers. As it turned out, I wore sports bras and "women's" underwear, which felt very comfortable. A year before I would become close to my first friend undergoing gender transition, and three years before my best friend would begin his transition, I learned that all of these years that my father never knew what I wore underneath my men's T-shirts and jeans.

My Mother

Mom bought our clothing as she stayed-at-home for a decade, cleaning our mud-stained clothes. Most often she listened to my sports league complaints while she served after-game dinner, typically oxtails, roast "beast," or spaghetti and "doo-doo balls." I usually grumbled about the competitive show-parents or schedule conflicts between soccer and basketball practices as my mom chopped and stirred at the stove

One time, however, I came home flustered and upset about recess. In my most composed-but-confused eight year-old recount, I explained that I was turned away from a school basketball game. A group of boys refused to let me join a team because I was a girl. It never occurred to me that being a girl made a difference about whether I could dribble, pass or shoot a basketball. Moreover, the more startling revelation was that others viewed me as a girl.

Until that point in my life, a mature second grader in my own mind, gender didn't seem like much other than a symbol that designated separate school bathrooms for those who preferred to pee sitting down or standing up. It was my first conscious encounter with the gender police who happen to be not much taller than four feet and were equipped with the only inflated recess basketball. The squad was mostly blond, and their chief, a loudmouth bossy kid marked the law: you're a girl, girls can't play basketball, and they especially can't play basketball with boys. My sophisticated reply: "that's dumb."

Gender logic never made sense to me: I was willing to concede that I was a girl but I also liked playing basketball and other sports for that matter. And importantly, it didn't seem fair. Why could they have the only recess basketball game? My righteous little-person moral compass decided that it could not stand. My mom, my greatest justice champion, lobbied the teacher on my behalf to let me play.

Once affirmative action got me into the game, I stayed in it. I dribbled, passed, and shot circles around the other players, apparently boys. From time to time, I grew tired of basketball at recess, so I enjoyed gossiping with other kids on the playground, apparently girls. I jumped back and forth between the blacktop and playground through sixth grade when our recess elementary fun ended. I didn't feel that my politics were too complicated, and I was satisfied that I was able to do what I wanted during the short periods of daytime that I wasn't in a "gifted" program or extra-curricular activity.

Interestingly, one important aspect of my appearance that allowed me to move between games was my hair. It was always in a short pony-tail that matched my boys' clothes. Every month mom drove me an hour and a half to a basement salon about 50 miles from my suburban enclave in poor southwest DC to visit Dru for my ritual perm. Dru was a tall imposing woman who always wore long skirts over her spotted shins, which resembled nickel pot-marks against her brown-yellow skin. She explained that the bruises littered along her lower legs were from her previous life as a young tomboy. I wasn't sure if that was true but I noticed the scars accumulating on my brown-yellow shins, and grew a little fearful that I would have permanent reminders of each playful fall, tumble, and fight.

Dru, like all Black hairdressers, offered us life advice. She and my mom would rattle the sinks with tales about the folks that they knew. As the news spread, over hot sauce soaked spare ribs if times were good, I would brace when she'd part my hair with a thin comb, and dump burning foam onto my scalp. It was the same every visit.

When I was 12 or so, on the edge of my final elementary school triumphs, she began to assure my mom that I would not stay a tomboy forever. She'd turn her head sideways to me and say, "Baby, you'll grow out of it…once you get interested in boys. You'll want to be pretty, and not be their friends anymore…"

Her promise was always sealed with a lump of foam slathered onto my broken-off hair. She'd deliver the same advice for five years. And on every visit, my hair resisted the gentle lie with each fiery follicle that reluctantly cracked from its natural kinky ribbon into a seared lifeless streak.

I was college-bound not long after my 18th birthday. I never saw Dru once I moved four hours away from where I grew up to the southeastern part of the state. I would never grow out of my tomboy phase either. I continued to flirt, date, and love women as I'd done for four years. About two years later, I would grow out my lifeless, broken-off permed hair, and another year later, I began to grow in my beautiful brown locks.

My Arrival

By my second-year of law school, I noticed that store clerks were confused. Some were even irritated that I would float from the Men's Section to the Women's Section, leisurely examining fits, feeling textures, and comparing sizes. Most also noticed my locks and kept their eyes on the bags that I carried.

I gradually learned that the clerks' expressions were distinct from my school friends' shocked looks when they learned about my occasional indulgence in, and secret joy of, French Manicures. My nails never lasted long because powerlifting ensured that they'd deteriorate within a week. Yet, at the same time, my friends' shock typically resembled the embarrassed looks of strangers, when they would call me "sir," or "brotha" on the street, only to see a feminine face when they pass by upon closer inspection. It was a winter-time pattern when onlookers were "deceived" by my bundled up body, wide stance, and stiff gait from far away. They would feel mistaken when they saw my finer facial features and almond eyes. My second-grade self never cared for the rules, and since queer liberation entered my post-college life, I generally made my own when it came to gender.

My partner at the time, a kind, white midwestern woman, was clearly attracted to my boyishness but seemingly preferred my physical femininity. She occasionally repeated a common refrain that I heard growing up from adults: "you're so pretty, why do you hide it with these clothes?" I explained, as best I could, that I'd always felt comfortable in my clothes.

My body's proportions were always a little

different in my mind's eye, after all. My chest wasn't as large; my shoulders broader; hips were rounder. Therefore, "men's clothes" were a better fit. On the other hand, men's clothes weren't made for my actual body, so I liked some "women's clothes," especially tops, because with the right cut, they held my C-sized breasts, yet showed my muscled chest. It was often a longer explanation than expected—complicated in a way, relatable in another.

As I re-defined my own gender rules, after 25 years, my identity became more fluid too. "Trans" was the identities of my best friends from high school and college, a description far outside of me. It inched closer as I looked into the mirror more to see a grown, and aging "tomboy." When I was in spaces in which folks bothered to ask, I started to express no preference about my gender pronouns—"he," was as fine as "she." I chose whichever "gender neutral" bathroom when they were available. Gradually, I replaced tomboy with "bi-gender," then "multi-gender," which was discarded for "genderqueer," which was before "genderfluid" made sense. I just knew that being perceived as a "woman" was never my reality ("lady" was the worst) and increasingly one that I was hesitant to accept.

My caring partner was quietly confused, like the store clerks, at these changes over three years. She loved my southern gentleman demeanor, its dignified chivalry and cool patience, with my clothes on. She also loved my full "feminine" hourglass figure, its athletic tone and delicate bones, with my clothes off. She and I grew to deeply love each other as we were, over the rough and tumble of law school, and life's changes as time passed. She and I though, were different in fundamental ways. She, for the most part, very much cared about the rules, and I simply didn't.

I could be one way with clothes on, and another way with clothes off, but maybe I couldn't be the same person at the same time. Her enthusiasm for my identity experiments faded; I spoke about "not being a woman" less when the label was put onto me.

Perhaps, as she grappled with her own sexuality boxes, it may have seemed unfair for me to choose many boxes or none at all. The funny thing was that she loved me too much but not enough at the same time. We grew too far apart, tried to reach for each other for too long, and our relationship ended too hard a year after we graduated together.

My Spirit-Sake

Shamanism is a compelling calling for a rule-breaker like me. The spirit world, as I experienced it, is infinitely more expansive and contains fewer boundaries than the "mundane" world. Medicine people, in particular, are called upon to travel spirit dimensions for messages, symbols, and other healing powers to ease our worldly suffering. Gender vagrants might be specially prepared to be empathetic healers given our in-between-ness in a gender regimented world. At the very least I like to think so.

In my spirit world experience, boxes are unnecessary—shamans are said to be hollow bones through which healing travels and sound conduits should not be so easily contained. The human experience seems less harsh when nature is your prototype. With Earth as a divine teacher, structural tensions are as natural as tree knots, and change flows as effortlessly as the water that constitutes our bodies. It is an awareness of our existence that is more forgiving of ambiguity, certainly more than law practice. I play on both sides, I am encased by my own skin, I am many and none at all, and it is here that I met him, a special spirit guide.

His Name Is Dirt. We met a short time ago on a spiritual journey to the upper-world. He tells me that "dirt" is a rough translation of a much more beautiful name in another language. He explains that the Earth which describes his name is much like clay. His power derives from the warm redness of the Earth.

Dirt is painter and dancer. He arrives to me in two forms: either he is wildly flicking large pots into the air, scrawling thick bands of grainy syrup-paste, like paint, across his invisible canvas. Or he is in spirit dance, adored with a few pieces of bright cloth and bone pieces, pounding his legs, pushing his chest, and angling his arms to the innate hard-drum rhythms.

He is proud to be my gender-keeper and creative source. His energy is of a "masculine" spirit—but not entirely. He also is the holder of the Sacred Feminine, our primal singularity with Earth-Mother. As my captivating spirit guide, he embodies the union of beauty and power, complementary and essential to one another. He is Passion. He is Wild. He is Exquisite. He is Powerful.

He is a part of me. Dirt is one reflection of my true self. My mirror of resilience that resists being cut and diced into the gendered world; my snarky echo with an attitude too unencumbered to care about controlling imagination; my holy connection so vibrant that it stays rooted in my deepest natural rhythms. His spirit serves not only as inspiration for transcending mundane gendered life—he validates my existence as a multi-elemental being made of divine substance and power.

Myself

My day-to-day life as a queer gentleboi of color is made a little bit easier with a spiritual companion. I'm not forced to routinely make tough choices about safety or to constantly correct pronouns or to always brave verbal abuse every day, unlike many genderqueer/trans-folks. The parts of my reality, however, which are layered with gendered alienation, queered outs, and hurtful assumptions, are anchored in love by my supportive family (blood and chosen) and communities. After 28 years, I'm learning that complex authenticity is held by a little girl playing in the dirt, and a big spirit playing in my heart. The mundane life is not much unlike the murky waters that I used to fish but my memories of freedom, and creative liberation, offer the clarity that I need for now.

-Richael Faithful

Healing

To my little Golden Boi. Baby Zahyr.

For reading while your 13 year-old hands clutch a 9-millimeter. Alone. In your room. In a dress.

You will be 29 years young someday. You will run out of draws. Your older brother will then give you a pair of his brand new, bright blue spandex fruit of the loom boxer briefs to tide you over til wash day. Your masculinity will no longer be a question.

YOU, are loved. It's not just what they tell you babe, it's what's true. Pain, is the only vacuous emotion in your universe right now. A heavy, quite endurance, is the sum of what you have known. But your rising star is built of flame and you will make it. Through this moment. Through this day.

And I get it. I understand. Some days, the pulpit swallows you up. Some of those who love you most, are preaching that your existence begs the creator's condemnation. That plain is a desolate one. The air is dry and suffocating there. No therapist, medicine, or mutilation can walk with you there.

Walk with yourself. Back bent, war torn, hopeless and screaming. You will not be invisible forever.

Your broken open will help someone else's blooming. Those voices advocating for the trigger won't warn you of the crushing of your mother. Bible in her hand. Maybe you don't care right now, but understand that it's complicated.

I get it. You feel like you have crushed her already. What wedding, of whose daughter, will she attend now? Who will bear the grandchildren? What kind of shame have you forced upon her? Yours is a family cloaked in the teachings of God's word. YOU, are a Sun. Buttoned down and bleeding light you are amongst the gifted whose feet grow heavy as they walk amongst the holy.

I get it. If nothing you do will ever be enough to right the wrong of how you love, then let the gun residue coat your hands and welcome the eternal resting of your mind.

Don't go just yet young one.

There will always be blood in that corridor babe

Many among us have died there after being taught to hate ourselves.

Stay true to living. And if you are lucky, the blood you did not shed will fill the cups of those spirits who reflect yours for generations to come.

You are loved. Your village is pure.

Let me tell you of the love I know now. That of your mother. Grasping Jehovah as she may, her feet have traveled a million mountaintops so that you would not have to live with your shoulders hunched in shame of your own shadow. Your mother is one without venom. Someday your mother will greet you while you are wearing wingtips and she will say, "I should have had a boy. I was going to name you Wesley." You will feel proud in that moment. That in her own way, she see's you.

On this woman's shoulders you will continue to stand. And she will continue to breath confidence in you without restraint. You will live for the moments where she laughs, gut busting with pride in your accomplishments. You will cherish those slumber parties, where you huddled, knees pressed against hers, watching endless episodes of *The Twilight Zone*.

Your father will call you Zay. Cause that's how he says your name. In his own way, he will advise you as his youngest son.

Your brothers will dance at your wedding when it comes. They will be your best men. They will see you. And when they do, they will pass down their crowns and lift you up. Proud of their young one. Their baby boi. Their transmasculine bloodline blood and bone. The fourth, and youngest Prince.

You are loved. Your village is pure. Many who remain unnamed here will brace your legs when your body is weak and your mind ragged from questioning your right to exist. They will be your 33. The fortification of your spine.

Young Boi, you will never be alone. You will weep. And you will tell no one now. But soon you will realize there is kinship to be found in this struggle. There is a flowering there. A celebration of kindred boihood roots.

Your village is pure. With love, they will embrace and encourage you just as you are. And you must remember, that these reflections of you, this village of yours, will be your molding. Your comfort. Your space to fall into and your community to make proud.

Finally, always remember, that no matter the

scripture, that woman, and all those who love you, never gave you up.

I get it. It's complicated. But hold on. Hang on. Breath deep. Stay the course. And carry on. Whether you see it or not, in this space, you are blooming.

Love,
Zah

-Zahyr Lauren

Bandages

He was beautiful, with an oily smoothness. I could—did—spend hours admiring him as he worked. I envied the tip of his tongue as it traced his upper lip, gazed at the curve of his neck as he bent over a notebook, and resisted the urge to run my fingers over every notch in his spine. He was nothing if not masculine, and yet he was all curves: curves of smiles and laughs, curves of hips and breasts.

The breasts. Every morning he bandaged them down. He used to glare into the mirror as he yanked the Ace bandage across his chest. The more he glared, the more he hated seeing himself, until finally he only stared at his feet—not just when bandaging his chest, but all the time, as if preserving masculinity by avoiding eye contact.

Outside of the bedroom, he wore an undershirt and a T-shirt and a button-up beneath a sweater, hiding his chest behind a wall of clothes. But in the bedroom, he stripped down and let my eyes devour him. I feasted on the hills of his breasts and the flat, hairless plains of his stomach. I rested my hands on the hips that held up sagging, washed-out boxers. When he stood up, I kissed his kneecaps.

"You're a man," I said.

I wanted to say, "You're beautiful," but he would have scowled, closed off and shriveled up. The words stayed curled beneath my tongue.

-J. Tomas

I Learned it from Watching You: Performing Masculinity while Unlearning Patriarchy

"Who taught you to hate yourself?" Malcolm's words had me locked into his 1962 speech, hungry for more of his anti-white supremacy shade. At the time I was a daughter of the "golden era" of hip-hop and Public Enemy, X-Clan and Boogie Down Productions were heavily involved with the shaping of my critical consciousness. Notice all of the men I've mentioned as being a part of my development?

I grew up in California, a certified tomboy. I was the fastest girl on my track team, the best break dancer in my crew, the dopest rapper in the cypher. I was one of the best boys I had ever met. But when we started exploring our little sexual selves, I noticed a small tingling in my body that happened every time I had a sleepover at a girl's house. The tingle was somehow related to the feeling I got when watching Prince videos, particularly the inexplicable yumminess I felt from Wendy and Lisa. The way they swayed together in unison to the Minneapolis sound was similar to the humping my friends and I would do when parents left us to our own devices. This was 1984 and crack cocaine had landed in my neighborhood, in my house. Many parents were suspiciously gone at night and us kids found comfort and normalcy in each other, chosen family.

"Is the water warm enough? Yes Lisa. Shall we begin?"

Whatever this was it felt gloriously nasty, a love lesson from residents of 'Erotic City.' What water? Begin what? Long story short, I decided they were together and I wanted in, or at least my own Wendy to run water for. Before I could make a move on the cute girl of my choice, the daughter of my mother's friend made a move on me. I spent the night at her house while our moms partied on the streets of LA. This girl, let's call her Keisha (realistic as hell for the Black Los Angeles 80s), started humping me in the middle of the night and as you can imagine, nightgown friction was in full effect. Acting surprised and protecting what little of my heterosexuality I owned, I demanded that she stop, while secretly hoping she'd continue. And continue she did. "The girls in my neighborhood do this all the time," she said. I remember feeling a sense of relief, humanized between disbelief and pleasure. From that point forward, I found girls my age from the block to 'do it' with and to my surprise, they were down. Here was yet another area of life where I outshone the boys.

When *The Color Purple* came out around this time (1985), I heard sound bites from the national debate about sexism and abuse within the Black community while hanging out at my 'big mama's' house. My grandmother, Ceola Nunn, migrated from Mississippi to Cali along with hundreds of thousands of others during the multi-decade great migration. She watched *Donahue* and *Oprah* religiously and stayed glued to the television trying to make sense of crack (several of her children were addicts), AIDs, hip-hop and Michael Jackson's rightfully outrageous popularity. The stench of Reaganomics had us all searching the TV guide for answers. These were the cultural forces that shaped my family during a critical time in my development. To complicate things more, Alice Walker brings Mister, Celie and Ms Sophia to an already chaotic and confusingly inspiring decade. But why were the Tony Browns, the Ishmael Reeds and the Farrakhans of the world upset with Alice? And what did they mean by "airing dirty laundry?"

We had lots of dirty laundry in my family, and more often than not it was related to men hurting women. My mother, my aunts, my grandmother all had secrets that came to life. More damaging for me to witness, as a kid, was men continuing this business with little accountability from the women. But women were not inherently cooperative and I know this now. They, too, were indoctrinated by this gendered political system that deemed them invisible—less valuable. bell hooks describes how embedded such a system is in the cultural practices of black life.

At church they had learned that God created man to rule the world and everything in it and that it was the work of women to help men perform these tasks, to obey, and to always assume a subordinate role in relation to a powerful man. They were taught that God was male. These teachings were reinforced in every institution they encountered--schools, courthouses, clubs, sports arenas, as well as churches. Embracing patriarchal thinking, like everyone else around them, they taught it to their children because it seemed like a "natural" way to organize life.

I decided on my own (consciously), that men were inherently abusive and dishonest, that's what being a man meant and decided (unconsciously) that perhaps that's what loving a woman meant? It took years and reading the work of Audre Lorde, Patricia Hill Collins, Mark Anthony Neal and so many others, to move from using terms like sexism and masculinity to describe a political system that felt much larger than these words could hold. These scholars/artists gave me the word patriarchy and still, I saw no place where I could in fact be someone carrying out its order, hadn't yet noticed my ability to outshine the boys in this area of life as well.

I was excited to have an opinion about *The Color Purple*, an opinion based on personal experiences. Alice Walker was telling the truth and not enough of us had the tools to understand it. I was shielded from the film because of its heavy sexual content. Little did my family know, my peers and I were sexually active, even if we were fully clothed, and by that time, like Shug, I was exploring my desire for girls and boys. But when I was old enough to watch it, maybe five years later, it became especially clear that I was also a victim of abuse—and not simply parental discipline otherwise known as spanking. My father would explode when triggered and typically my mother and I were the first available for the anger's landing. I have two sisters, but my older sister lived separately from us and my youngest sister was barely five at the time. The brunt of that rage found time on my body. Middle child blues, I bore witness. My mother's drug use intensified before a divorce happened and I was left to piece together a story that would allow me to understand and survive—or better yet, react to this unsolicited truth. I had little access to what loving someone well meant. From this space, I stepped into a vicious multi-decade cycle of painful love suffering.

I screened "The Color Purple 30 Years Later" in Atlanta, Georgia and posed the question to a mainly lesbian and queer identified audience. "Who taught you how to love women?" Because if the answer is men, then depending on what the men in your family did, some of us were in trouble. "Who taught you to hate women?" is another way to frame the question, pulling on the same Socratic method that Malcolm did, probing the audience to go further into critical thought about ways we learn to love.

Alice's work also had me thinking about radical change as a possibility for everyone. The film encourages reflection on the work that must be done to investigate the context of behavior, so as to avoid demonizing and dehumanizing folks when working towards interrupting the cycle of abuse. Since then, with an open heart, I have watched my father, like Mister, become a gentle, remorseful and loving man and I have watched my mother reach each year of sobriety with dignity. We are not a broken people.

The decision to unlearn patriarchal masculinity has been/will be a journey. After moving in and out of abusive/dysfunctional partnerships, I've finally landed in a space where I can see my pattern and build a way out of it. I have the honor to be working directly with Dr. bell hooks and be in conversation with her about what unlearning patriarchal masculinity looks like in real time. Some of those conversations look like me pushing back on recent comments she's made that could be seen as ideas that uphold patriarchal masculinity. The biggest, most valuable lesson here is that absolutely nobody is perfect, but we owe it to each other to provide safe spaces to learn. I'm proud of where I am now, a place that makes the forgiveness of myself for harming others and forgiving those (family and former lovers) who have harmed me necessary for my healing. To find this forgiveness I had to first admit to myself, then to my partner, then to the public, that I have been, at times, a womanist and a womanizer, a healer and a heartbreaker, a conscious and controlling human being in relationship. I've partnered with women who have similar contradictions and patterns. In fact, many of the people I've partnered with have been survivors of childhood violence, have had a parent with an addiction and have had relationships where intimate partner violence existed—painful love suffering. Like me, some of these magical women have been powerful forces in the community, with a touch of madness that complicates their public, personal and political identities.

We attract people who reflect where we are, and because I wasn't ready to look at myself, I kept selecting partners who showed me, by mirroring aspects of my own behavior, the work I needed to do. We triggered each other sometimes to the point of violence, in every sense of the word. My hope is that they, too, will share their history, so that transformative justice and community accountability is a process we all have access to, a process that is detached from the desire to control the narrative of the ending of a relationship. This truth telling will encourage less shame around finding the support we need to be in right relationship with each other and create less space for demonizing people who do struggle to be their whole selves in love. I strongly believe that abuse in the queer community should be reviewed with a unique and specialized lens. It requires a nuanced discussion that works to understand the entanglement of verbal, emotional and psychological abuse that creates the conditions for a mutually abusive dynamic. We cannot afford to give into the rigidity of a victim/perpetrator binary; there are far too many stories within the story for us.

It is through radical self-awareness, energy healing practices, and a partner whose work is rooted in complexity, compassion and the creation of alternative realities that I have begun the work to unlearn abusive behavior. I will spend the rest of my life committed to being whole, working to bring together the schisms that threaten my peace and stability and the peace and stability of women I love.

I share this while holding the understanding that ancestral and familial trauma, the war on drugs, mass incarceration, anger, race rage, domestic and state sanctioned violence showed up in my life, shaping me, before I learned to speak. The hurt from it stayed lodged in my body as untreated trauma until I had enough tools to begin the healing journey.

Brooklyn-based journalist Esther Armah describes this struggle powerfully, asserting that, "Trauma cannot be treated by legislation or ideology alone—no matter its power. It is neither political, ideological, or philosophical. It is emotional. Emotionality masquerading as ideology creates cyclical arguments that end in hurt feelings, repeated individual narratives, exchange of insults, imploding organizations and untouched institutional power. Platforms alone were just never enough. We needed process. Why? Some wounds we buried. Some wounds buried us. We became living graveyards. We carried bodies and bones in our living bodies and our bones." The fact is, none of us can escape patriarchal conditioning and 'the farming of bones,' but learning that I have other choices to give and receive the love I deserve, I have found my relationship with masculinity to be a less charged and quite frankly a less hurtful experience for those who invite me into their heart space.

I possess two gender spirits (out of the many available to us) that I'm in deep relationship with and at deep peace with. I am a Black woman who enjoys performing masculinity and I do it well. More accurately, I'm a fag. Born in 1975, I'm a 80s baby type of gender bender and it's taken me years to 'wake up like this,' fully comfortable in my body and excited about the skin it's in. I now see masculinity as an extension of my style, as an expression of my layered identity, and as an opportunity to revise masculinity in a way that feels empowering to all who come into contact with it. It's a conscious way to perform my personality and my taste, and this performance is finally, or should I say constantly, because I'm a damn work in progress, one that cultivates the parts of myself that are not rooted in trauma, but in transformative love.

-Lynnée Denise

Dear Baby Jazmine

You don't know me yet, but you will. We are not the same; but we, without a doubt, are one. I am writing this letter to you, to warn you about your truth-by telling you about my truth. Eventually it will be your truth as well, but until then—enjoy what you think is your truth. (Who knows, this may be my truth only for the moment).

* * *

For years I never really understood my truth. My truth always seemed to be determined by what everyone else's truth was. It was as if society, before I sneezed my first achoo, had this idea of everything that I was supposed to be, what I was supposed to eat and even who I was supposed to love. The interesting part was…no one asked me what my truth was.

I was told for almost 19 years that my truth was that I was a girl/woman. Along with that truth came the preconceived idea of womanhood; pink frilly laced dresses, HER, emotional nights worrying about where my man was, SHE, lying to seem powerless resulting in intense amounts of submission. I tried it, well tried being the feminine woman that society thought was the correct way for me to be. That is not me; it was someone else's truth. I even tried to deconstruct the idea of being a feminine woman. I tried to develop a truth that allowed being androgynous or masculine and still being a woman to be acceptable. My tight pants that had my signature sag, accompanied by tight graphic tees that let the world know that my truth was still "I am a woman" was mixed in with pressed khakis, ties and dress shirts. Permed hair transitioned to FroHawks and wavy low cuts. But my truth was still that I was a woman, masculine, but a woman nonetheless.. Society's idea of what a woman was (masculine or not) still did not match who I saw myself as when I looked in the mirror. When I looked in the mirror "She" and "Her" were nowhere to be found. Since I did not fit the truth that was given to me by society, maybe I was the truth that was given to my brothers…that I was a man.

For a few years I walked through my journey of life, following the truth that I told myself "I am a man." I walked with the "He's" and "Him's" of the world. For years, I even peed with them. While the words fit me more than when my truth was defined as a woman, the process did not fit me. The preconceived ideas of what a man was, what a Black man was, did not fit me. I was told that as a Black man, I had to exert unnecessary amounts of authority and power to get where I wanted to be. I had to always fight (whether physically or mentally) my Black masculine brothers and sisters. I had to be a boss. If I was anything less than a protector or a provider to my family, I was less than a man. Naturally, I could not be what was/is defined as a Black man. I could make myself physically into a man. I could take testosterone or get surgeries so that my body fit what a man's is; facial hair, a deep voice, and a serious amount of muscle mass.

But it was not a natural process that I was willing to endure. Now don't get the wrong idea, I have met many people throughout my journey who really are men that need to be self-made and by no means am I trying to dis their transition for it is one of the beautiful transitions of life. But, my truth is not their truth.

See Jazmine, I did not fit what a woman of any race, culture, or ethnicity was defined as by society; but I really could not fit the requirements that came with being a Black man. Naturally, I did not fit into any of the truths that were presented to me. I also was incapable of forcing myself into either one of them. I was trying to force a free spirit into all of these rules and requirements. I was trying to make a person who would rather sit on the fence and see both sides, pick a side and stay there for the rest of my life.

All of it made me question what my truth really is. My truth came in 2014, in the form of a Facebook gender pronoun. My truth finally had a name. My truth was transmasculine. The one thing that I love the most about myself is my masculinity. It has always been natural for me to be masculine. Even when I identified as a woman, my masculinity is what I valued the most. I always felt uncomfortable in practices where femininity was more prevalent than masculinity. I can be masculine and still keep my baby face, no shaving needed. I can be masculine and still have emotional nights worrying about where my partner is, which is seen as a feminine thing for some reason. My truth allows me to have characteristics of both women and men in the most natural form. My masculinity allows me to be seen as just Jazz, not as a man nor a woman. My truth allows me to be Sir both with a sports bra on, as well as a binder to conceal my chest. My masculinity encourages me to go to the gym and develop my muscles alongside both men and women. My masculine identity is not forced to fit what the world knows to be masculine. On top of all of that, I can make my own definition of what transmasculine is because the definition is so ambiguous. For me it means that I transitioned from a feminine human with my point in transition being a masculine human.

This is my truth. I am neither a man nor a woman. I am a proud transmasculine hybrid human whose masculinity is rooted deep in my center.

But that is not the end of this understanding of this truth. But one of the most interesting parts about accepting, loving, and understanding my truth is the liberty that came with it. Without constricting myself to a man or a woman, I feel more comfortable about exposing the few feminine traits that I have. Before the little femininity I had was looked down upon because of patriarchy (when my truth was a woman) or emasculation (when my truth was that I was a man). Now I accept and embrace that part of me because even the most masculine people have some femininity in them, femininity that should not evoke shame. I am a living example that some people really do not fit in a binary but instead operate on a spectrum or even a kaleidoscope.

Jazmine, I am your truth, just as you are my truth. We are all truths that are loved without shame for they taught us and made us who we were, are and will be.

Continue learning about your truth baby!

Always loving you,
Not-So-Adult Jazz

-Jazz Jordan

Mismanaged Masculinity or, "Why I Stayed"

#whyistayed

Because I had intentionally chosen him. I chose him for his alpha male motions. His hard-edged, right to the point notions. Because I wanted someone more masculine than myself, and for the past year had been proclaiming "Sigh. Even daddies need a daddy." I wanted a Daddy to take initiative, to be the creative one that came up with plans, to handle me. I wanted a Daddy so that I could be the Boy for a change. And so that I could work on my own issues of mismanaged masculinity through experiencing someone more dude-lier than me.

I stayed because he was further along in his medical transition than me. Because he had smooth facial hair, a baritone voice, and muscular pecs. Because he was read as male always and in all places and together we would present as two gay men. This presentation was so affirming to me as a masculine person with long-standing attractions to other masculine of center people. It made me feel most inside of my full queer self.

I stayed because similar to cis-men I had dated in the past, he too was obsessed with the mechanics of music. I could talk about genres of music, instrumentation and of singers. But he was in the male-dominated world of sound engineering and could break down digital techniques of mixing, mastering and audio boards. How hot.

I stayed because we had a connection. We could talk for hours about everything, something, and nothing at all. Because we laughed, a lot, and hard. In spite of all of our differences we created a venn diagram of unity when it came to race, being transmen, and our love of music and spirit. He was interested in my healing practices and what it meant for me to be two-spirit. In that respect he was supportive of my wellness.

Finally, I stayed because he was making changes. He was starting to talk more than yell. He was starting to engage rather than shutting down. He was starting to find humility vs. defensiveness. He really was. But really… really… really slowly.

#whyileft

I left the first time because right before my first acupuncture appointment (something I was nervous and delicate about), he cussed at me. And when the needles broke my skin, all his words and expletives really sunk in. And the weeks of supreme shade were illuminated at that moment.

I left because he was homophobic. He swore up and down that he didn't like guys, that he only liked me. To add, I wasn't just the Boy and he the Daddy, I was also body hairless, still had my breasts, my voice slightly less deep and to him my stage of transitioning was comforting because then he could pretend he was actually still with a woman. He would whine when I spoke of medically transitioning. He passed judgment upon the emotional sensitivities of my gay male friends, and attributed their emotiveness to them being feminine and gay.

I left because he confused my need for communication with "trying to soften him up." As a social worker, a two-spirit person, and as an activist, my communication skills are on point. They were threatening to him. Strong communication is a necessity to me for any relationship, especially a polyamorous relationship, and especially during conflict. In modeling healthy communication, I was accused of being condescending. In encouraging healthy communication, he would shut down. He also insisted on a moratorium of bringing up issues that had previously been discussed. His minimizing of communication was like asking me not to sleep or to not digest my food. Thus I was left tired and hungry.

I left the final time because ultimately he was also transphobic. In our last fight I encouraged him to look within and to engage in deep self-reflection for answers to the issues between us. In response, he texted, "Yea, whatever chick." He knew that these would be some of the most hurtful words I could hear, but I don't think he realized that in that statement he was playing the "Will the real trans person stand up" game. A game that is rooted in cis-centered heteronormative patriarchal notions of realness and respectability. Yea, then I was done.

#laterinlife

After the final break-up, he consulted one of our older trans uncle figures who tore into him about his problematic words and actions. And to him he listened. He continued having conversations with other transmen and slowly started to realize the err of his ways. We spoke for the first time about seven months after the last break-up and he was super apologetic. He had learned the value of communication and about how deep his internalized homophobia and transphobia was. He seemed more patient and reflective. He had in fact changed a lot. We started hanging out a bit again. I was cautious, and rightfully so, because while change does happen, he had gone from zero to about 60, and not to 100 as he purported. And ain't nobody got time for that. So I set a strong boundary that for the first time he actually respected.

Now we are cordial and only text occasionally. And I do miss him at times, our laughter and conversation, and the amazing sex. And while this Daddy would still love a Daddy, I realize I don't want someone that is reminiscent of my real daddy. I know the signs now too. I know the implications inferred in those who don't hear you, and can't look at themselves. Those that fear the identity attached to their practices. Those that run and are afraid to walk, yell and are scared to talk.

Finally, in the end I did learn a lot about my own mismanaged masculinity. Areas where I used to and could potentially still show up just like him. I no longer demonize him, rather I see myself as a reflection. A reflection of an image of a man gone wrong. The foolishness with him actually helped bolster my own feminism, and further even helped me identify my own areas of fierce femmeness. The femme in me is helping the rest of me to find comfort in stillness, rather than defaulting to action. The femme in me has presented a beautiful paradox of actually helping me to be the man I want to be. One who honors intentional observation along with informed participation. My two-spirit self is more balanced. And for that and other things, I am at peace for staying when I did, I am grateful that I left, and I am enlightened by the life lessons.

-Holiday Simmons

Black Bois Queering

I've always been the kind of lesbian-identified person to explicitly declare my love for black women. Beautiful women just command my attention. I'm the kind to fall in love at least once a day off of aesthetics alone. I'm the pro-black lesbian. I love creating a place of love between sistas because black women are discarded in our society. I've always thought this was a special place to share an intimacy with someone who could truly understand the complexities of blackness, queerness and womanhood because they lived it too.

As I hold space for these women and continue to grow, my sense of responsibility to this ideal deepens. But as of late I've found myself not being accountable to the true healing and acceptance that needs to happen in these spaces. The black women I adore, actually deserve more than I can give them. And I've had to look into myself to figure out how. It's hard enough wanting to hold a healing space when you yourself are not healing first. This is my struggle to heal the masculinity within me.

Healing Masculinity

Black and Queer Bois are an easy target. We stand out in a world that accepts queerness and blackness and womanhood only on certain bodies. I wonder what it means to hold all of these, and to exalt a black masculinity that is so different in its dangers.

Even as a woman-identified person, when black masculinity rests on this body, it's encased in stereotypes of black manhood. Through queering my masculinity, I'm forced to reexamine long- held standards of black masculinity. And daily I'm forced to reconcile the womanism and queerness of confronting my misogyny, and that other feeling of grasping for any connection or community in this broken world.

Black masculinity to me is much more than stripes and signifiers, yet I don't always treat it that way. I'm learning to bend my own rules a little more, to be less critical with myself first. That way I can give the femininity in my life more space, the space we all need.

Our masculinity doesn't want this. Black masculinity in America has always been a devoted tool of patriarchy. As the rule it was created to aspire to white masculinity, and to uplift white femininity. This Black Boi can't do either without leaving some fundamental parts of myself behind.

In the end I'm constantly re-negotiating what it means to come correct, and to bring my best self to any relationship. As a black woman, this is hardest for me, because I've been taught to shrink myself for others. Though having a masculine presence means I can wake up as big as I need to, the demure still exists as a default.

Queering Humanity

In an ideal version of queering humanity, I'll be harnessing the feminine aspects of my brown self. My queerness will allow for growth and reflection and nurturing and different kinds of strength. But white patriarchy wants a black maleness for the Queer Boi that competes with whiteness. It wants a black womanhood that devalues black womanhood.

The deepest problem is patriarchy. When Black Bois fall into this trap, we perpetuate the destructiveness of masculinity. When we're not careful, we reinforce cycles of oppression within our own communities. I've done it recently. I front for myself, thinking that my misogyny is better coming from another woman, but I still have the privilege of walking home at night and not hearing cat-calls and not feeling the very real danger of rape.

So there's a part of me that is *still patriarchy, still ready to protect or at least deflect when I assume women I don't even know are threatened. That's the part that's really rooted in an understanding of the danger from outside. But in relationships it's harder, because there's also a feminine part of me, being bullied by my masculinity. That masculinity builds walls and creates barriers to healing and love.

So, to claim my identity as a place of healing between black women I now understand is somehow disingenuous. That makes me understand black masculinity even more. That gives me the space and the reason to claim healing for myself first. That makes my masculinity my problem and my goal. I want a Black and Queer Boi masculinity that is

314

defined by the love for black womanhood that I've always felt it to be.

I want my masculinity to work for community, for relationships, for the world in a way that allows rather than restricts. The standards of masculinity, as set by white men have backfired, tremendously. No one can live up to them because they've been quantified... as money, as status, as notches on a belt, as prestige.

Black Boi and Still Woman

The Black Boi sits in a very crucial and dark and powerful corner in our communities. I think about the history of black womanhood, and the history of black masculinity and there is something of a pattern to the way they've been structured to compete in this society. Black women in our history have used masculinity and queerness as a disguise to get out of trouble or to make trouble. Think the Blues Women who stood on stage and ballooned themselves while exposing white patriarchy in post-slavery America.

Black masculinity was forced into a hierarchy that serves white supremacy and oppresses black womanhood. So, for black women taking up a masculine of center presence there's a sense of power in this picture. At least in my version. I see this space where I sit and am self-determining my relationship to blackness in a queer-as hell combination of once 'powerless' racial identities.

Though I'm still exploring what it means in the many different contexts where I exist I know masculinity as a valuable part of my expression. As

315

masculine presenting as I am, I still get to be soft as hell. I can still ask for and appreciate affection. I am soft and caring. So at the end of the day the appearance of masculinity is another survival mechanism of queerness. We must remember that the master's tools ain't gonna bring shit down. Our compliance with hetero-patriarchal masculinity ain't going to queer it. Our resistance to the necessity of masculinity won't either. Only our devotion to bringing balance in ourselves will.

-Eledeah Clack

Brotherboy

I am an Aboriginal Australian, my skin my not be dark in colour but my heart is black through and through. I am proud of my black heritage because it is the oldest living culture to date, dating back to further than 60,000 BC. My great grandmother is from the Wakka Wakka nation and her partner, my great grandfather, is from the Wulli Wulli nation. My totem is the Tawny Frogmouth bird, they live up in the high trees and keep a close eye on everything. I find myself analysing fine details most of the time, especially my own body.

I've always known I was different from a young age, going out to dance I'd feel uncomfortable being with the girls and seeing my little boy cousins learning men's dance. It actually made me quite gloomy inside, now that I reflect on it. I've stopped dancing now.. Dysphoria has been quite grappling.

When I was 11, I started cutting myself because I hated what my body was doing to me and how my guy mates were treating me because of the changes that were starting to happen. Luckily they weren't bad cuts, so they've all faded away now. When I was 13, I started getting into drugs and alcohol which is already a bad problem in aboriginal communities but I really capitalised on it. I hated myself so much for the changes I was going through and, to top it off, I was sexually assaulted. I tried committing suicide three times that year. That case has been unresolved as a result of the justice system that works against young "girls," especially aboriginal ones.

When I was 15, I was sent to Catholic school to straighten myself out. This is where I became immersed in my studies and started to learn a lot in class. My favourite subjects in high school were Ancient History, English and Film. In my final year of school, I was one of the school captains and got a full scholarship to one of Australia's most prestigious universities. At university, this is when I started to become myself and discover who I truly was. A young man, hiding inside this body of a female, was ready to come out and show the world what he has.

At first, beginning my transition made me feel extremely disconnected from my culture. Because I did not know of any Brotherboy in Australia, only heard of Sistergirls. I was so unsure if my culture would accommodate my gender identity, so I ran away from home early 2014 back to my traditional country (Wakka Wakka and Wulli Wullli) to find answers.

I sat down with an elder to discuss what I've been going through and she listened to me and wished me well. That relieved a lot of the anxiety that was flashing through my body at the time. I then went on to drive further away to see my father and tell him about my decision to medically transition and start hormones. I knew this would be a significant milestone in my transition. He couldn't hold back his emotions and just cried and cried and cried. It made me feel somewhat guilty but I knew he was happy for me and that was the reason why he was crying. My father is my rock, I've never told him this, but I know he is aware that he is my rock. He is the one who blessed me with the blood I carry, the family name 60,000 years old.

I started networking on Facebook and found a group Sistergirls and Brotherboys Australia. This was a group for other aboriginal gender diverse people like me. I am so grateful I found these mob on Facebook because without them, I'd be so lost without my culture or uncomfortable in the wrong body. The people on the page are like my family, they call me their bubba. I recently stayed in a household with two transgender people (1 Sistergirl and her ftm partner) from the page, that are parents to a little girl. Their family is the most gorgeous little family, full of radiance and good energy. We spent the weekend recording a video resource which we are launching at a conference in Sydney. It will be the first video of its kind discussing what it means to be Brotherboy. If I had this resource, it would have guided me so much through my transition but I am also glad to be the first person to put it out there.

My dream is to start cultural dancing again, I stopped because men traditionally dance with no shirt on and paint their totem on their chest. When I get top surgery, I pray and hope to Biami (our creator) that I will be able to dance again. Being cultural keeps me strong spiritually and being Brotherboy, living in my true gender, keeps me strong mentally. Then I can pass these things onto my kids who will bare their family name and a rich knowledge of their culture and who they are.

-Kai Clancy

My Back is Strong: Navigating Healing through Black Masculinity/Femininity

*My body carries within its frame beauty and agony...
I've learned to accept it, as is... I was steadily
reaching in the dark across a chasm that separated
who I was and who I should be. Somewhere along the
way, I grew weary of grasping at possible selves, just
out of reach. So I put my arms down and wrapped
them around me. I began healing by embracing myself.*
-**Janet Mock**; *Redefining Realness*

The image that comes before this embrace, this self-acceptance—that constant grabbing at distant, perfect images of the self—looks like something else to me. It reminds me of surrender. But surrendering to what?

The thing that caught me off guard as a Black boi reading Mock's autobiography is what shocks me about all the life narratives I come across: how similar we are. In little and big ways. From habits to ideologies. The abuses we've faced. When I bought *Redefining Realness* at the Northeast LGBT Conference, I found myself unable to form words in her presence as she signed my copy, because she still seemed an idol. I question how I could have so much in common with someone I hold in such high regard, someone seemingly unbreakable to me. And then, I think again, about those imagined, perfected selves we tend to grasp toward. How often I chastise myself for not being "there" yet (and "there" sometimes changes its place, remaining ever elusive).

And then I realize that what I consume in those grasping moments is a subtle and idealized self-hatred. What I am surrendering to are ideas whispered to me about who is good enough, and how I need to alter my Self in order to be more valuable, more validated. And it's not as easily identifiable as aspiring toward white supremacist standards of beauty. I think it's easy to forget the ways systems of exclusion and domination are at work in even radical spaces, in queer and Black spaces—that there is a certain "look" to legitimized identity, legitimized boihood.

Gravity gives the appearance of working in the opposite direction here. There is so much I have to struggle against, that I have to fight with all my might against to finally put my arms down, to stop surrendering, to embrace myself.

There is so much work necessary in loving who I am. Not who I am told to be, not even who I want to be, not a potential self. But who I am, right now. With noticeable flaws and all. Battling with what parts of my femininity to hold on to, which ones to release. With feelings of isolation and inadequacy. Putting forth the labor to recover from past abuses. That is the me that I have to embrace, the one I am working to love.

I learned from bell hooks that radical self-love is a necessity for appropriately loving others. But this has become more than a means to an end for me, more than a stepping stone toward the "real goal" of loving others. I have to see the capacity of loving myself as a worthy goal all on its own.

My ability to be gentle, kind, and forgiving to myself—skills not taught to Black folks in white supremacist society—cannot be a side-step towards becoming fit for the prize of large scale revolution. First, because I think it an obvious mistake to discuss movement building in capitalistic terms, like a commodity to be earned where your capacity for vulnerability, theoretical knowledge, and fashion sense count as currency. Let me simplify the idea by saying this: the revolution is not for sale.

Second, I think there lies some embarrassment for masculine-of-center folks in admitting that there is a need to work towards self-love. That there is a need to heal from (even decades old) wounds. It comes from and is fed by a cultural cynicism, the hardening factor of masculinity. That fear of admitting victimhood, the fear that acknowledging the need for healing is weakness. And the belief that weakness is an undesirable human trait, a feminine trait. There is hardly any space for accountability and interdependence, so is it not somewhat futile to work towards improving yourself in that way? Shouldn't you be putting your effort in something a little more productive?

Then again, I cannot simply wait for the tide of the world to shift before taking my own survival seriously. And, to be quite honest, I'm bored and exhausted with the idea that working on your Self constitutes navel gazing and a waste of time. These are messages that kept me from seriously considering my own need to heal for quite some time. Especially when you're swallowing messages about the dichotomous nature of femininity and masculinity. And especially when giving into femininity ain't going to help you make it in this world.

Perhaps I forgot at some point that I don't want to "make it" in the world as it is. I hope to make the world softer so that it has room for me, all of me, and others who are struggling against themSelves without stopping to acknowledge why.

As it is said, change begins in the self. I have to take the initiative. I am the one who has to make room for all of me first. I cannot help anyone else and I cannot help carry them. My back is strong enough to carry my load - believe me, that's more than enough weight. But in doing that, in embracing myself, I can feel the world soften around me because I am healing and changing within it.

-Che Justus

Navigating Masculinity as a Black Transman: "I will never straighten out my wrist."

"Straighten out your wrist, Brotha!" When my boxing coach yelled these words, I knew his call was about more than perfecting my jab. I have experienced the demands of Black masculinity and the responses to my failure to perform properly are not all that different from the experiences of failed masculinity that I felt within Black lesbian communities. But it is true, I am now a young Black American Male. People usually assume that I am somewhere between the age of 15 and 20. I'm 28.

The world is unkind to Black bois. The world is unkind to Black girls. But the way our gendered bodies are policed is different. Black bois are assumed thugs, thieves, rapists, and overly-aggressive. I knew this already, but I feel it more now like when I got kicked out of a Hollywood store because the owner assumed I was there to steal something. He didn't just make that assumption. This white man came over and hovered over me yelling for me to get out and to never return because "he knew my kind." I spoke calmly, but he kept yelling. I couldn't help but think, "this man can't see or hear me." He could only see what he believed to be true about young black bois, and it didn't matter who I was, who I had been, or who I might become. My future and past were predetermined in his mind. I was the dangerous body that needed to be policed.

And Black women have it too. Bearing the brunt of pathology, the Black woman has been told that she is the reason why Black people suffer. Because she has been too strong and emasculating. Because she is crazy and angry. She needs to be put in her place by Black men and those outside her racialized community. When my boxing coach told me to straighten out my wrist, it came after lots of criticism around my push-up form, my strength (or weakness). The way my body moved was sub-par especially in comparison to this ripped Black man. I have gone from being a big, strong looking Black woman to occupying the body of a young, lanky Black man. The more my body masculinizes, the more I feel my femininity stands out as contradictory to those who invest in normative types of masculinity.

So What is Masculinity? How Did I Come To Learn How To Wear It?

When I was in high school, I learned there was a code to same gender loving life. You were either masculine or femme, a stud or her girlfriend. I was told that my look was confusing.

People couldn't tell what I was. Someone told me that I was sporty "femme." I didn't know what that meant but I was happy that I had a name to call myself, a place to belong. The first woman I ever went on a date with was masculine presenting, a stud. She had a way of making me feel her masculinity as a direct opposite to my femininity. I didn't like the room I was given to move or to not move. I know that this interaction was circumscribed by chivalry. She opened my door and closed it. She paid for dinner. Something about this interaction made me feel trapped. I decided that I would be nobody's femme and therefore I must be like her, a masculine woman, a stud. I wanted to be in control.

I took the summer to learn my gendered role. I became a stud. And it worked because I was able to get the attention of the femmes that I was attracted to. In those early teenage years, I mostly learned from other studs how to be. I remember the first time I learned about stud misogyny. I was 18 or 19 at the time and I was at a house party in the Bay Area. There were many beautiful Black women in the space. There were studs and femmes. The host was a stud who wore cornrows, baggy jeans, and perhaps a polo or a jersey. She was good looking, but somehow I knew that was something I wasn't supposed to articulate aloud. I remember looking at her and examining the family photos that had been on display in her house. The girl in the picture was different. She was femme. She smiled. I wondered if the girl in the picture felt like she needed more room. I wondered if the stud she had become gave her more room. I wondered how that room, that liberation that she felt came from dominating feminine women or perhaps the feminine that might have been a part of her.

I remember walking in on a conversation between two studs. One told the story of how her girlfriend broke her chain and how upset she was. The other stud chimed in, "If that had been my girl, I would have slapped her." Everyone laughed, but I was afraid. That's probably one of the earliest moments that I felt uneasy about being a stud and the kind of masculinity we were creating and inheriting. Another lesson in studly masculinity came for me when I was in college. I had fallen for an older femme woman. We'd spend time walking and holding hands in the New England chill.

She taught me how to be a good stud.

"You should always walk on this side of the street, so that I feel protected."

"You should always open the door for the lady."

I was getting schooled in old-fashioned chivalry and I was good at it. I was in love with it. The giving, the idea that I could somehow protect. But it wasn't simply that I could protect. There was an insistence that I MUST. Anything else meant failure. What if I was afraid? What if I needed to feel/be protected? Well, that was the sacrifice of normative masculinity.

After I had top-surgery, I needed help with my carry-on bags when flying. I wasn't able to raise my arms above my head. No one could see that I needed help. I didn't have any visible wounds, so I had to ask. I asked a white stewardess for help and she glared at me. She was annoyed and she didn't want to help me. I explained to her that I had just had surgery and still annoyed, she told me that next time I would need to check my bag if I couldn't do it myself. I was a young, seemingly able-bodied Black man. I wasn't elderly. Why did I need help?

How can we expect to create healthy men and bois, if they live in a society where asking for help is met with punishment and enforced shame? Is there room for vulnerability in masculinity? We must make room.

Who I Am Today

I walk in the world today as an effeminate Black transman. Queer, indeed! I never want to straighten out my wrist. I want it to flare, I want it to paint flame across canvas because I am unafraid of femininity. It is the place from which I garner my strength.

The term Masculine of Center has been one that I have clung to for sometime now.

Masculine of center (MOC) coined by B. Cole of the Brown Boi Project, recognizes the breadth and depth of identity for lesbian/queer/womyn who tilt toward the masculine side of the gender scale and includes a wide range of identities such as butch, stud, aggressive/AG, dom, macha, tomboi, trans-masculine etc. When I discovered it, I thought, "Finally, a term that can hold me!" But as I sit here today and write, my center feels feminine. Is there room for that? We must make it.

I have always carried with me both masculine and feminine energies, but I have often been forced to choose one over the other depending upon the space around me.

I have been on hormones since July 2011. I had top surgery in May 2012. It is 2013 and while some things have clearly changed physically and emotionally, some things have stayed the same. I still bleed every month. For many, this may seem to be a contradiction to my masculinity or maleness, but I cherish the moments.

I am thankful that my body carries both masculinity and femininity at its core, because at the end of the day, what we should all be striving towards is balance. We need to build relationships between men and women that allow space for both parties to grow. We need to build relationships between men and men, women and women, that allow space for both parties to move freely. The gender binary affects us all in detrimental ways. And while masculinity may seem to offer more room, it also has its limitations. And femininity, if only understood as masculinity's property, is detrimental to women and other people who identify as femme. Hi, my name is Kai M. Green. I am a Black Transman. I am a Black feminist and my center is just as feminine as it is Black.

Who I Am Today 2015

I am a Black Transman and the way I walk in the world changes. If I'm with my queer, more-or-less femme partner, we are usually read as a heterosexual couple. When walking alone, I have heard the word "faggot" tossed my way more than once, probably because sometimes if I'm not thinking about it, I can let my hips sway freely and hands swing, feeling oh so pretty and gay, but the streets aren't always safe so I know how to adjust. I do not bleed every month. My skin and face are just as smooth as they were two years ago, even though I keep wishing for this shadow to yield to the stache. I said before that I would never straighten my wrist. I lied.

While riding the train with one of my best male friends he made himself vulnerable, and in that vulnerability he reached for my hand, and before he could grab hold, I pulled back quickly. I checked to see if anyone had been watching. All of this happened and it seemed automatic. I did not want anyone to think that we were gay, that we were anything more than two dudes riding a train. I was afraid that we, that I, might be subject to some kind of homophobic violence, something that might land and sting much harder than the passing "faggot." So I yanked my hand away. Hurt, I looked in my friends eyes, I had surprised us both.

Hi, my name is Kai M. Green. I am a Black Transman. I am a Black feminist and my center is just as feminine as it is Black. I am struggling with my internalized homophobia, which for me, I think, stems from a fear of a loss of masculine privilege. To reach back and hold my brother's hand in public without fear is what I long to be courageous enough to do. But I am not there. I still have work to do. So sometimes I straighten out my wrist. Sometimes I butch up my stride so that my walk is just a little bit easier, safer, but I know this is not the end. Being able to fit in, to move in line with, to assume a heteronormative position is not going to make more space for me or others who perhaps don't have the option or desire to fit in. They say you should never say never and I understand that more now. I want to live in a world where I don't have to remember to straighten my wrist or regulate the sway of my hips. I understand now that that work requires a commitment to changing the world, but it also requires a continuous commitment to undoing the world that lives in me—internalized homophobia, transphobia, ableism—for it keeps me from fully loving myself and my brothers. And if I'm in a world where I am unable to fully love, then surely I'm in a world where I cannot fully live.

-Dr Kai Green

Search for Home

Fear shows it's face in many of forms,
Sometimes in arrogance and egotisms
A false sense of self love and respect
Man plays GOD, the very essence of light and existence
Man created man and woman, man created oppression
and idealism
We created hatred and war, we left peace in search of
power
We abide by the laws of "The Creator"
We {adapt} to society's norms
But some of us are beyond Ancient, we are timeless
souls that walk with unrest
Dalai Lamas
We are not to meant to be confined by mere man made
limits

R.I.P to all our warriors that has passed to pave our way

I refuse to allow you to let me suffer
I refuse to let me hate myself
I idolized my fathers,
I looked at Mogli, at Atreu
I believed, I was not complete, I am not whole

I imagined brothers, tall, handsome, lean and muscular
with big penises and pretty women
I needed escape, outside my reality, outside my skin
There is no way in hell, on earth, or in heaven that I
could be a WOMAN
I have breast, ovaries, womb, vagina, heightened
emotion, round face
There is no way in hell, on earth, or in heaven that I
could be a MAN
I am lost…
A lie to your civilization
I am wrong! I need to be fixed
Spiritually or physically
It's either/or
Religion or surgery

R.I.P to all our warriors that have passed to pave our way

Spirit does not tell me to end it all
To slit my wrists, to fall
I tell myself that, the conscience you have created as
God
Spirit tells me I'm beautiful in my bronze skin,
powerful with my ejaculating clit
My breast provides food for thought
So you tell me GOD
Am I not the man that every man dreamt of being?
That every woman wants?
Am I your opponent?
Your fallen angel?
Am I Lucifer's protégé?
I never wanted your Garden, but behold your followers
Who makes the rules to control my life

Who keeps my soul in a cage and turned it into a wild
beast
Are they not you?
Did man come from man?
Is it true that we're extra terrestrials that life that has
not originated from you?

I will not allow you to not let me find home

GOD I will not allow you to keep us in hiding.

-Akila Stewart

Secrets of a Brown Boi

To my fellow Brown Bois, studs, and masculine of center females remember to always strive for a healthy, positive, and spiritually inclined life. Be strong, be sweet, be respectful, be humble, take care of your woman, and love her everyday that you are blessed with.

Here is my survivor story of emotional, mental, and physical abuse.

The first incident
She threw a freezing cold cherry limeade slushy at my face

The second incident
She poured bottles of water on the interior of my car

The third incident
She shattered my windshield from the passenger side with her foot

The fourth incident
She spit right in my face, with malicious intent

<u>The fifth incident</u>
She took my keys
Left my car unlocked
Forced me to walk miles
And wait hours until I could have retrieve them after
three hours of begging

<u>The sixth incident</u>
She followed me home
Wrecked her car
Begged me to go back home with her
I refused
She scratched my face and took my glasses

<u>The seventh incident</u>
Those glasses she took
Well, she destroyed them
Rather ran over them with her car

<u>The eighth and ninth incidents</u>
She posted my number on *Craigslist*
Saying I was selling an iPhone or had free toilet paper
Damn
My phone was being blown up for days

<u>The tenth incident</u>
She clocked me with her elbow
For Thanksgiving I had a black eye

<u>The 11th incident</u>
She punched me in the nose
I couldn't breathe for days

The 12th incident
She posted me on *Craigslist* again
This time it was a sex ad
Fuck
I had to change my number
Block over 300 calls and texts messages

The 13th incident
I left my keys in her car while at the Courthouse
She wouldn't give them back
I stood by her car, we had a vicious exchange of words
20 cops intervened
They helped me retrieve my keys from her glove
compartment

The 14th incident
She threw a Java Chip Frappuccino on the roof of my
car

The Last Incident
I was at her apartment
She told me to leave
I did
She stopped me at the doorway
Slapped me across the face
My glasses flew off
She grabbed them and threw them outside

After every incident she would tell me the same shit.
I love you
I'll never do this again
I was drunk
It was the mary jane

I have a lot of issues
I need you
I'll die without you

Sometimes we would cry together
Other times we would have passionate make-up sex.
Damn.
Why did I have to be so addicted to her pussy?
Why did sex have to be so good?
She always laid it down on me

That last incident was when I was done
I had enough
I left after years of abuse.
I'm not a victim,
but a survivor

Just because I'm a brown boi doesn't mean that I'm not prone to domestic violence. I was trapped in a cycle. I was in a stranglehold of manipulation. I was in an unhealthy relationship. I stayed true to myself, never retaliating in a negative manner or stoop to her level.

I didn't know how to let go, how to leave, how to be alone, how to save myself. This female that I loved, spent so much time, money and energy on just destroyed my life. I allowed her to. I tried to save her so many times but by doing so I was killing myself.

This type of relationship is in our community
It's happening to our fellow brown bois, studs, butch females right now.

My familia, my boihood
Míra
Open your eyes
Wake up
We cannot keep domestic violence a secret anymore.
Our stories must be told to save, help, support and create a safe space for our fellow brown bois.

-Cassandra Mendez

An open letter to my public washroom gawkers.

It's ok, you don't need to check the sign on the door again, you are in the right bathroom, although you believe I am not.

The question is asked again, am I more uncomfortable than you? Are you more uncomfortable than me? The latter is most often the case. There, there, I know it's scary when not everything fits into the little boxes you and so many others have constructed in their heads, fighting and protesting to assert they are real, and all that there is. There, there, I don't bite. I do however: Love, feel, run, jump, eat, sleep, bleed, mourn, thrive, achieve, cry, laugh, fight, celebrate, enjoy, hurt, and swim. Just like you. Or do you for some reason believe that you and your ways are all that there is and we are not similar?

Ego.

Ego is what is wrong with everything. Of course there can be good kinds of ego, but the one I speak of leads to hate, discrimination, ignorance, and pain.

Ego is what gives you the false idea that everything should be the way you think it should be.

Shame on you.

Shame on humans.

On a larger scale the only thing that stops there being life elsewhere in the universe is our ego. Imaginary, and deep down unstable.

Ego is what tells you in your closed mind that male and female are all there is. Ego doesn't only mean what we think. Ego creates fear, control, manipulation, and scars. Scars hidden behind the ego or created by it?

Ego is what tells you I should have long hair, sit with my legs closed, have a different career, and drive a different car. A car you're ok with. One that won't go faster than yours.

Ego is fear. Fear of loss of control, fear of the unknown, and lack of comfort in oneself. For a (human) race who prides itself on being fearless....it's is quite evident this is not the case. Admitting your flaws will make you less flawed. Admitting you're wrong can make you less wrong, and admitting your way isn't all that exists will create a better world.

Ego.

This is not just about my appearance.

-Dani Bundy

Closing Note/Acknowledgements

We would like to say thank you to every contributor who rode this journey out with us and kept the energy and excitement up as we navigated the new field of publishing. For everyone who checked in on the progress of the collection, asked us how they could help, and who did help: thank you. To Asher Kolieboi for doing some initial gathering and consistently checking in with love: thank you. Thank you to each of the collective members who contributed past and present, including Jackie Fontaine and Genesis Tramaine. We're grateful to our volunteers and extremely supportive communities: Brooklyn, Detroit, Boston, Toronto, Philly, the Bay, internationally in Germany, Brazil, South Africa, Finland, the Philippines and beyond.

We also would like to send our grateful energy to our elders and ancestors who have set the tone for our work and progress.

And most gracious thanks to Riverside Books/Magnus for putting this thang in action.
We love y'all.

Queers out.

-the bois

About the Authors

bklyn boihood is Brooklyn-based, national collective that organizes events, collaborations, workshops, media projects dedicated to embracing the diaspora of masculinity in queer and trans bois of color.

Our mission is to support ourselves and our communities as we collectively redefine queer masculinity through storytelling, community-building and adventure crafting.

Core members (2016): Chino Hardin, Van Bailey, Morgan Mann Willis, Ryann Holmes and Zahyr Lauren.

Learn more about our work: www.bklynboihood.com

If you liked this, consider these other titles from Riverdale Avenue Books

Queering Sexual Violence: Radical Voice from Within the Anti-Violence Movement
Edited by Jennifer Patterson

Finding Masculinity:
Female to Male Transition in Adulthood
By Alexander Walker, Emmett J.P. Lundberg

Bi Any Other Name:
Bisexual People Speak Out
By Lani Ka'ahumanu, Loraine Hutchins

Queer Theory, Gender Theory:
An Instant Primer
By Riki Wilchins

Read My Lips:
Sexual Subversion and the End of Gender
By Riki Wilchins

Two Spirits, One Heart:
A Mother, Her Transgender Son and Their Journey to Love and Acceptance
By Marsha Aizumi, Aiden Takeo Aizumi